Islamic Atomic Bomb Cookbook

Fartash Barvarz

Order this book online at www.trafford.com
or email orders@trafford.com

Most Trafford titles are also available at major online book retailers.

Printed in Victoria, BC, Canada.

ISBN: 978-1-4269-2366-1

Library of Congress Control Number: 2009913595

*Our mission is to efficiently provide the world's finest, most comprehensive book publishing
service, enabling every author to experience success. To find out how to publish your
book, your way, and have it available worldwide, visit us online at www.trafford.com*

Trafford rev. 12/23/2009

 www.trafford.com

North America & international
toll-free: 1 888 232 4444 (USA & Canada)
phone: 250 383 6864 ♦ fax: 812 355 4082

Dedicated to Oleg Penkovsky

Oleg Vladimirovich Penkovsky, codenamed "Agent Hero" (Russian: Олег Владимирович Пеньковский; April 23, 1919, Vladikavkaz, North Ossetia, Soviet Russia, – May 16, 1963, Soviet Union), was a colonel with Soviet military intelligence (GRU) in the late 1950s and early 1960s who informed the United States about the Soviet Union placing missiles on Cuba, which led to the Cuban Missile Crisis.

Soviet leadership started the deployment of nuclear missiles in the belief that Washington would not detect the Cuban missile sites until it was too late to do anything about them. Penkovsky provided plans and descriptions of the nuclear rocket launch sites on Cuba. Only this information allowed the west to identify the missile sites from the low-resolution pictures provided by US U-2 spy planes.

Table of Contents

Introduction

Relations between Iran and Pakistan improved since after the removal of Taliban in 2002, but regional rivalry continues. Sunni-majority Pakistan sides with fellow Sunni Muslim Saudi Arabia in its competition with Shiite majority Iran for influence across the broader Islamic world, although Pakistan is far less ideological than either country, and is more concerned with influence in Central Asia rather than in the Arab world. Iran considers northern and western Afghanistan as its sphere of influence since its population is Persian Dari speaking. Pakistan considers southern and eastern Afghanistan as its sphere of influence since it is Pashto and Baloch speaking like the North-West Frontier Province and Pakistani Baluchistan, respectively. Pakistan expressed concern over India's plan to build a highway linking the southern Afghanistan city of Kandahar to Zahidan, since it will reduce Afghanistan's dependence on Pakistan to the benefit of Iran. There are still sporadic incidents of attacks on Pakistani Shi'as and allegations that Pakistan is attempting to change the demographic balance of the Northern Areas.

Both the countries joined the Economic Cooperation Organization (ECO), a derivative of Regional Co-operation for Development (RCD), which was established in 1964. The ECO groups neighboring non-Arab Muslim states. As part of this regional organizational framework both countries continue to cooperate on trade and investment.

In 2005, Iran and Pakistan conducted US$500 million of trade. The land border at Taftan is the conduit for trade in electricity and oil. Iran is extending its railway network towards Taftan but the gauges are of different sizes, 1435 mm and 1676 mm respectively.

It is estimated that there are approximately 10,000-20,000 centrifuges in Kahuta. This means that with P2 machines, they would be producing between 75–100 kg of HEU since 1986, when full production of weapons-grade HEU began. Also the production of HEU was voluntarily capped by Pakistan between 1991 and 1997, and the five nuclear tests of 28 May 1998 also consumed HEU. So it is safe to assume that between 1986 and 2005 (prior to the 2005 earthquake), KRL produced 1500 kg of HEU. Accounting for losses in the production of weapons, it can be assumed that each weapon would need 20 kg of HEU; sufficient for 75 bombs as in 2005.

It was confirmed that Pakistan has built Soviet-style road-mobile missiles, state-of-the-art air defenses around strategic sites, and other concealment measures. Pakistan has also built hard and deeply buried storage and launch facilities to retain a second strike capability in case of a nuclear war. In 1998, Pakistan had 'at least six secret locations' and since then it is believed Pakistan may have many more such secret sites. In 2008, the United States admitted that it did not know where all of Pakistan's nuclear sites are located. Pakistani defense officials have continued to rebuff and deflect American requests for more details about the location and security of the country's nuclear sites.

Dr. Omidmehr and his visits

Dr. Ali Akbar Omid Mehr is an IRI diplomat that broke with the regime at last and found political shelter in Europe. He was a political analyst in the IRI consulate in Peshawar. In one of nuclear deals, Mr. Omid Mehr paid five million $ to one of Pakistani leader, when they were asking for twenty five million

$. After negotiating their accepted the price and everything and until this time Mr. Omid Mehr doesn't know what he's buying or what's going on.

After some time they parcel the package which makes him think maybe there are some books inside but he found out they are Uranium Mills which Islamic Republic ordered from Ukraine. No one actually knows the amount and numbers of other deals but Mr. Omid Mehr said at that time"Imagine If I bought five million $ Uranium for Iran by accident, then think about other deals with Iran's Northern countries. I cannot even imagine.

Sham Pasha was the Pakistani leader which they met for the deal with at that time. He is a regional leader which controls the area for themselves and made a huge black market for Drugs, Weapons and other stuff. He was the leader of seven tribe at that time.

Mr. Omid Mehr sent a telex to Dr Velayati and says my works are done and waiting for your permit make the deal. He got the reply on the telex so fast which contained these words.

"Buy it.

Dr Velayati "

That's how it was done.

Mr. Omid Mehr tried to meet with Bin Laden twice also from Iranian government. The first time, it was at 1990.Bin Laden had pretty good financial situation at that time and used to run his business also.

Anyhow he hadn't met with Mr. Omid Mehr at first time. As you know Iranian are Shi'as and they're Sunnis and that's kind of a big issue over there which roots in the history. Even almost at the same year Bin Laden's Hardliner Forces killed two Iranian Diplomats.

The 2nd time was at 1994 when Bin Laden was in trouble. They took his Passport and lost the business also. At the same time Saudi financial support was decreasing and all these put him in a difficult situation.

Mr. Omid Mehr says when Bin Laden sees him at the second time; he hugs Mr. Omid Mehr and takes him to a side to talk in privacy with him.

He said "we're really proud of our co operations and involvements which our Muslim brothers they are having with Iranian Trainees and Sepah. "He was acting so different at the 2nd time. Mr. Omid Mehr was not sure what's he's hearing or how to react.

Mr. Omid Mehr used to go to a Sheraton Hotel in Mary which they spend the weekends with his family. For reaching the Hotel, there was a pretty long road trip which goes through Islamabad Road. That particular weekend was The Day of Ashura which is a sob ceremony for Muslim which they all wear black, cry and sometimes even hit themselves and closes all the businesses and shops. The Ceremony has a religious history root for Muslims. Anyhow that weekend was pretty different a lot of youth they were partying, singing, dancing and celebrating with colorful clothes and when he reached to the hotel Abdul Qadeer Khan which was in the hotel already shake his hand and welcomed him. Qadeer khan told him Mr. Kashani is also upstairs. At that day he found out Iranian Authorities were providing funds and support to Abdul Qadeer Khan to start with the secret atomic tests which gave them experience and the knowledge.

In a meeting with former Pakistani president in his villa which Omid Mehr was there as the translator for Mr. Akhondzadeh.

Eshagh Khan suddenly said to Akhondzadeh that you have to thank the supreme Leader a lot for the 800 meters of land which you gave the control on. Always before our fishermen and traders had big problems and I promise you that we, Two Muslim Brothers Countries will make the first atomic nuclear bomb together. Mr. Akhondzadeh lost his temper so fast and became so angry why Eshagh Khan had talked when I was in the meeting.

Dr. Omid Mehr gave a 52Pages top secrets report about nuclear issue which he was gathering for four months before leaving, to Scandinavian countries Ambassadors and EU members.

Pakistan in the way

Pakistan, which is not a member of the Nuclear Non-Proliferation Treaty, has two nuclear reactors of 425 MW power to generate electricity. The third nuclear reactor will be operation in the spring of 2010. Pakistan began focusing on nuclear development in January 1972 in the regime of Prime Minister Zulfiqar Ali Bhutto, who delegated the program to nuclear scientists Munir Ahmad Khan, Abdul Qadeer Khan and military administrator General Zahid Ali Akbar.

In Pakistan, nuclear power makes a small contribution to total energy production and requirements, supplying only 2.34% of the country's electricity. Total generating capacity is 20 GWe and in 2006, 98 billion kWh gross was produced, 37% of it from gas, 29% from oil. The Pakistan Atomic Energy Commission (PAEC) is responsible for all nuclear energy and research applications in the country. The father of the first Islamic Atomic bomb also is a pakistanian, Abdul Qadeer Khan. He was the atomic scientist which co-operate with Iran and other Hardliner governments around the globe. Abdul Qadeer Khan, the Pakistani nuclear scientist at the centre of the world's largest proliferation scandal, has been freed from five years of house arrest by a court in Islamabad at February 2009. The High court rules Abdul Qadeer Khan was not involved in selling nuclear secrets to Iran, North Korea and Libya.

Khan, lionized as the "father" of Pakistan's atomic bomb, confessed in 2004 to selling nuclear secrets to Iran, North Korea and Libya. He was immediately pardoned but detained in his home.

The hero of Pakistan's nuclear weapons capability was born in present day India, in Bhopal State, in 1936 - the son of a teacher in a family of modest means. For five years, between the 1947 establishment of India as an independent state and 1952, Khan was a citizen of India. Then the Muslim Khan immigrated to Pakistan with his family as did millions of other Muslims before and after the 1947 partition of the two states. After graduating from school in Karachi he went to Europe in 1961 to continue his studies. First in Germany he attended the Technische Universität of West Berlin, then in Holland where he received a degree in metallurgical engineering at the Technical University of Delft in 1967. Eventually Khan received a Ph.D. in metallurgy from the Catholic University of Leuven in Belgium in 1972.

After graduation Khan went to work for the Physical Dynamics Research Laboratory (FDO), a subsidiary of Verenigde Machine-Fabrieken, in Amsterdam in May 1972. FDO was a subcontractor to Ultra-Centrifuge Nederland (UCN) - the Dutch partner of the tri-national European uranium enrichment centrifuge consortium URENCO, made up of Britain, Germany, and the Netherlands.

Since Khan had lived in Europe from 1961 on and was married to a Dutch national (as the Dutch security service BVD believed) the very personable Khan had little trouble getting a security clearance - a *limited* security clearance. Curiously Khan's wife

Henny was not Dutch though, but a Dutch-speaking South African holding a British passport.

Elementary principals of security were not, it seems, observed by any part of the URENCO establishment. Routine procedures, such as wearing identification badges marked with the level of clearance appear to have been unknown. Once someone gained access to part of a facility with one level of clearance, there seem to have been few if any barriers to moving to higher level areas. The customary practice of checking the security clearance level of a person before signing out to classified documents to them appears to have been ignored.

Within a week of starting with FDO A. Q. Khan was sent to the UCN enrichment facility in Almelo, Netherlands. A visit to an external facility would normally require the transmittal of security paperwork to be granted access. This procedure was ignored by both FDO and UCN, because Khan was not cleared to visit the UCN facility, though he would do so repeatedly during his employment.

The multi-lingual engineer was tasked with translating highly classified technical documents describing the centrifuges in detail. In the course of this work, he often took the documents home, with FDO's consent, even though this was also a breach of normal procedure. In his first two years Khan worked with two early centrifuge designs, the CNOR and SNOR machines, then in late 1974 UCN asked Khan to translate highly classified design documents for two advanced German machines, the G-1 and G-2. These represented the most sophisticated industrial enrichment technology in the world at the time.

Khan spent 16 days over the course of a month in the highest security area of the Almelo facility while studying these machines. During this period he had unsupervised access, and was noted roaming around, writing notes in a foreign script, but with the lax security culture no attempts to stop him or investigate his activities.

A.Q. Khan initially worked under the Pakistan Atomic Energy Commission (PAEC), headed by Munir Ahmad Khan. A small centrifuge pilot facility was initially set up at Sihala, several kilometers southeast of Islamabad. Friction quickly developed and in July 1976 Bhutto gave Khan autonomous control of the uranium enrichment project, reporting directly to the Prime Minister's office, an arrangement that has continued since. A.Q. Khan founded the Engineering Research Laboratories (ERL) on 31 July 1976, a few kilometers from Sihala, outside Kahuta near Islamabad, with the exclusive task of indigenous development of Uranium Enrichment Plant. Construction on Pakistan's first centrifuges began that year. The PAEC under M. A. Khan went on to develop Pakistan's first generation of nuclear weapons in the 1980s

Due to Khan's efforts, the slow recognition of the program by western intelligence, and the weak export controls at the time, Pakistan made rapid progress in developing U-235 production capability. When export controls on nuclear usable materials were imposed on Pakistan in 1974, the focus was on technology applicable to plutonium production, not uranium enrichment, and the focus was on plants and complete systems, not components. By using Khan's detailed information of components and suppliers Pakistan was able to circumvent these controls.

According to Khan in a 1998 interview, the first enrichment was done at Kahuta on 4 April 1978. The plant was made operational in 1979 and by 1981 was producing substantial quantities of uranium.

In recognition of A. Q. Khan's contributions the ERL was renamed the A.Q. Khan Research Laboratories (KRL) by President Zia ul-Haq on 1 May 1981.

A later Dutch security enquiry revealed that Khan had probably appropriated much of the UCN facility's secrets. Starting in 1978, he was also named in numerous other Western inquiries and media reports about secret purchasing operations for components for Pakistan's uranium enrichment plant.

Khan acknowledges he did take advantage of his experience of many years of working on similar projects in Europe and his contacts there with various manufacturing firms, but denies engaging in nuclear espionage for which a court in Amsterdam sentenced him in absentia in 1983 to four years in prison. An appeals court two years later upheld his appeal against the conviction and quashed the sentence for failure to properly deliver a summons to him.

The prosecution had the option to renew the charges and issue a fresh summons for trial, but given the impossibility of serving him a summons behind the curtain of Pakistani security the Dutch government decided against pursuing the case any further - a fact that Khan claims as an admission that there was no substance to the case.

"The information I had asked for was ordinary technical information available in published literature for many decades," Khan said in a speech afterwards about his two letters to his contacts that became the basis for his prosecution.

"I had requested for it as we had no library of our own at that time."

Of course the classified documents he undoubtedly copied and sent to Pakistan, as well as his written notes were not in the possession of Dutch security and thus could not be used to build a case against him.

Khan insists that the Pakistani centrifuge program is indigenous and that the equipment used in it was developed and manufactured locally. In 1990 Khan declared "All the research work was the result of our innovation and struggle. We did not receive any technical know-how from abroad, but we can't reject the use of books, magazines and research papers in this connection."

It has been reported that a CIA analyses of Pakistan's huge purchasing program showed that they had succeeded in obtaining at least one of almost every component needed to build a centrifuge enrichment plant.

The notion - expressed by Khan - that his personal access to detailed classified and proprietary ultracentrifuge designs was coincidental to his role in leading Pakistan's enrichment program, that he declined to employ the knowledge he had gained at FDO to assist Pakistan's program in constructing an enrichment plant in five years, and that the wholesale importation of the entire technology suite required to build a European-designed centrifuge plant does not constitute "technical know-how from abroad" cannot be taken seriously, to say the least.

The massive purchases of foreign equipment - continuing up through the purchase of ring magnets from China in the mid-90s, show heavy dependence on foreign technology and components. But even so, the plants themselves are Pakistani developments -- Pakistan had to design and build the facilities, assemble the systems from components, while manufacturing components themselves that they could not obtain in sufficient number. This is quite unlike reactors and plutonium separation plants that other proliferating countries have acquired ready-made and were trained to operate by their suppliers.

Khan, because of the secrecy enveloping Pakistan's nuclear program, has lived heavily guarded by security men. Over the years there have been a number of incidents involving encounters between foreigners and the heavy-handed security surrounding Khan and KRL. In late July 1979, unidentified men stopped and beat severely the French Ambassador and his First Secretary as they were driving by Khan's laboratories in Kahuta. A few weeks later in August a journalist for the *Financial Times* named Chris Sherwell trying to locate Khan's house to conduct an interview in Islamabad was beaten up and then arrested and charged with fictitious crimes, forcing him to leave the country. Later a British diplomat's son was detained by police after losing his way in the Islamabad district that houses Khan.

Despite the secrecy and security, Khan has taken the public spotlight on numerous occasions, attracting some criticism for seeking publicity in contrast to his more discrete counterpart in India, Abdul Kalam.

It was on such an occasion - an interview in February 1984 - that he first made the claim that Pakistan had achieved nuclear weapons capability.

And when the 1986-87 Exercise Brasstacks crisis was at its height on 28 January 1987 - an outbreak of warfare between India and Pakistan seemed imminent due to a confrontation over military exercises near the border - A.Q. Khan made threatening remarks regarding Pakistani nuclear retaliation to Indian journalist Kuldip Nayar, apparently intending that they be conveyed to the Indian government. Nayar however shopped the story around for a few weeks, and it was not published until 1 March, after the matter had been resolved. Nonetheless it left a lingering sense of nuclear threat with India.

Khan's public pronouncements also helped generate the tense atmosphere in which India's 1998 nuclear tests were conducted. In an inauspiciously timed visit, Bill Richardson led a high level U.S. delegation that visited New Delhi and then Pakistan on 15 April. During the visit Khan, told the Urdu daily *Ausaf* "We are ready to carry out nuclear explosion anytime and the day this political decision will be made, we will show the world," during an informal chat with journalists. "We have achieved uranium enrichment capability way back in 1978 and after that several times we asked different governments to grant us permission to carry out a nuclear test. But we did not get the permission," the daily quoted him as saying. Asked when Pakistan would carry out a nuclear test, Dr. Khan was quoted as having said, "Get permission from the government." Khan was not a spokesman for the government at the time, but he remained extremely influential and was still closely connected with the corridors of power in Pakistan.

As a result, not everyone in Pakistan holds Khan in awe. Some who have worked with him remember him as a egomaniacal lightweight given to exaggerating his expertise. "Most of the scientists who work on weapons are serious. They are sobered by the weight of what they don't know," said Munir Ahmad Khan, the former head of the PAEC. "Khan is a showman."

Despite his extreme prominence (Khan is one of the most famous men in Pakistan) and undoubted importance in Pakistan's acquisition of nuclear weapons, A. Q. Khan was never in charge of the actual development of nuclear weapons themselves (despite common assumptions to the contrary, which Khan did nothing to discourage). Weapons development, and their eventual testing, was carried out by the PAEC.

During the 1990s Khan lived in a spacious single-story house, located in Islamabad near the Faisal mosque, with his wife Henny and two daughters. The road outside his house is a public thoroughfare, but there are safety bumps in the road surface to slow traffic and a permanent security post is opposite the house. On the road, his car is escorted by four-wheel drive security vehicles with sirens and lights blaring and flashing.

Khan keeps a small menagerie of pets. Each day at sunrise, he takes a sackful of peanuts when he walks into the wooded Margala Hills across from his home and feeds the monkeys. Declared Khan, the day after his country exploded another nuclear device, "I am the kindest man in Pakistan. I feed the ants in the morning. I feed the monkeys."

At 1997 Khan begin to transfer centrifuges and centrifuges components to Libya. Libya received 20 assembled centrifuges and components for 200 additional units for a pilot enrichment facility. Khan's network will continue to supply centrifuges components until late 2003.

At 1998 India detonate a total of five devices in nuclear tests on May11, 13. Pakistan responds with six nuclear tests on May 28, 30.

At 1999 Pakistan government released an advertisement of procedures for the export of nuclear equipments and components. The Ad listed equipment for sale, including gas centrifuges and Magnet baffles for enriching uranium. Other advertisements from KRL are reported to include an "unsubtle drawing" of a mushroom cloud and Vacuum devices that attach to centrifuge casings.

Abdul Qadeer Khan's official career came to an abrupt end in March 2001, when he and PAEC Chairman Ishfaq Ahmed were suddenly retired by order of General (and now President) Pervez Musharraf. What prompted this move can only be speculated, but the Pakistani weapons program - which has been sponsored, run, and controlled by the military from its outset - is now mature, and it may be that Musharraf, who was busy mending fences with the outside world, wished to tie down some loose cannons that were a source of irritation with India and the United States. Both men were offered the post of "adviser to the chief executive", which Khan eventually rejected after much vacillation. Khan is now described as "Special Adviser to the Chief Executive on Strategic and KRL Affairs" a wholly ceremonial title.

At 2004 Khan makes a public confession on Pakistani Television of his illegal nuclear dealings in English. He claimed that he initiated the transfers and cites an "Error of Judgment". He is pardoned soon after the President Musharaf and has been under house arrest since. The Pakistani government said khan acted independently and without state of knowledge.

At March 2004, a container aboard the BBC china (the ship that was previously intercepted) arrives in Libya with one additional container of P-2 centrifuges components. Colonel Qaddafi reports the arrival to American Intelligent and the IAEA. Libyans warns Americans officials that not all of the components from Libya's orders had arrived and some might still show up in the future.

In a letter that Khan sent to British journalist Simon Henderson, parts of which have already been made public with the latest dribble coming out ahead of Obama's visit to China in November 2009, the Pakistani metallurgist reveals the following sequence of an episode the broad contours of which are well known despite Chinese-Pakistani subterfuge for nearly 30 years: In 1976, some four years after India tested its first nuclear device, Pakistan's then Prime Minister Zulfikar Ali Bhutto approached China's supreme leader Chairman Mao in his quest for the nuclear bomb. By this time, Bhutto had already invited expat Pakistani scientists, including A.Q.Khan, to return home to help Islamabad make the bomb to ensure that the country was never again humiliated by India the way it happened in 1971.

Mao died soon after, but according to Khan, the matter was advanced in talks he and two other Pakistani officials, including then foreign secretary Agha Shahi, had with Chinese officials at Mao's funeral. It was not a one-sided transaction: the Pakistanis told the Chinese how European-designed centrifuges (whose designs Khan had stolen) could swiftly aid China's lagging uranium-enrichment program.

"Chinese experts started coming regularly to learn the whole technology" from Pakistan and Pakistani experts were dispatched to Hanzhong in central China, where they helped "put up a centrifuge plant," Khan said in an account he gave to his wife after Musharraf purged him under US pressure. That letter eventually found its way to the Henderson who shared it with the Washington Post, which advanced the story on Thursday. "We sent 135 C-130 plane loads of machines, inverters, valves, flow meters, pressure gauges," Khan wrote. "Our teams stayed there for weeks to help and their teams stayed here for weeks at a time."

Initially, it appears China sent Pakistan 15 tons of uranium hexafluoride (UF6), a feedstock for Pakistan's centrifuges that Khan's colleagues were having difficulty producing on their own. Evidently, Khan had made the centrifuges from the designs he stole but did not have enough raw materials to run it. Khan said the gas enabled the laboratory to begin producing bomb-grade uranium in 1982. Chinese scientists also helped the Pakistanis solve other nuclear weapons challenges.

By then, Gen.Zia-ul Haq had taken over the resigns in Islamabad and had hanged Bhutto. Rumors of a pre-emptive strike by India and Israel on Pakistan's nuclear program rattled Zia, who sent Khan and an unnamed Pakistani general to Beijing with a request in mid-1982 to borrow enough bomb-grade uranium for a few weapons.

After winning Chinese leader Deng Xiaoping's approval, Khan, the general and two others flew aboard a US made Pakistani C-130 to Urumqi. Khan says they enjoyed barbecued lamb while waiting for the Chinese military to pack the small uranium bricks into lead-lined boxes, 10 single-kilogram ingots to a box for a total of 50 kilograms of highly enriched uranium (HEU), for the flight back to Islamabad. "The Chinese gave us drawings of the nuclear weapon, gave us kg50 enriched uranium," Khan wrote in letter to his wife Henny which was meant to be an expose to get even with the military, which locked him up on proliferation charges even though Khan says they were part of the transactions approved by all governments that came to power in Islamabad, civilian or military.

By Khan's account, Pakistan did not initially use the Chinese fissile material and kept it in storage till 1985 because they had made a "few bombs" with their own material. The Pakistanis then asked Beijing if it wanted its nuclear material back. After a few days, Khan says the Chinese wrote back "that the HEU loaned earlier was now to be considered as a gift... in gratitude" for Pakistani help. The Pakistanis promptly used the Chinese material to fabricate hemispheres for two weapons and added them to Pakistan's arsenal.

Khan sees this act of stealing, begging and borrowing to make the bomb as a supreme accomplishment by Pakistan. "The speed of our work and our achievements surprised our worst enemies and adversaries and the West stood helplessly by to see a Third World nation, unable even to produce bicycle chains or sewing needles, mastering the most advanced nuclear technology in the shortest possible span of time," he boasts in a separate 11-page narrative that the Post said he wrote for Pakistani intelligence officials.

Aircraft -The Pakistan Air Force (PAF) is believed to have practised "toss-bombing" in the 1990s, a method of launching weapons from fighter-bombers which can also be used to deliver nuclear warheads. The PAF has two units (No. 16 Sqn and No. 26 Sqn) operating around 50 of the Chinese-built Nanchang A-5C, believed to be the preferred vehicle for delivery of nuclear weapons due to its long range. The others are various variants of the Dassault Mirage III and Dassault Mirage 5, of which around 156 are currently operated by the Pakistan Air Force. The PAF also operates some 46 F-16 fighters, the first 32 of which were delivered in the 1980s and believed by some to have been modified for nuclear weapons delivery.

It has also been reported that an air-launched cruise missile (ALCM) with a range of 350 km has been developed by Pakistan, designated Hatf 8 and named Ra'ad ALCM, which may theoretically be armed with a nuclear warhead. It was reported to have been test-fired by a Dassault Mirage III fighter and, according to one Western official, is believed to be capable of penetrating some air defense/missile defense systems.

India's nuclear programs

The father of India's nuclear research programs, the founder-director of the Tata Institute of Fundamental Research (TIFR), the founder-chairman of India's Atomic Energy Commission, the moving spirit behind India's space and nuclear weapons programs and the founder of the country's first nuclear reactor and power station, Homi Jehangir Bhabha (1909-1966) is one of the visionary leaders of India's creditable progress in science and technology. When the World War broke out he was in India and he accepted an invitation from Dr. C.V. Raman, Nobel Laureate, to join the Indian Institute of Science in Bangalore, founded and headed by him. Dr. Bhabha accepted the invitation of the great scientist and joined the Institute as the head of its newly formed Cosmic Ray Research Unit (1939). TIFR came into being in 1945, and the Atomic energy Commission of India was set up in 1948. Dr. Bhabha represented India in International Atomic Energy Forums, and was President of the UN Conference on the Peaceful Uses of Atomic energy in Geneva, Switzerland in 1955. He served as member of the Indian Cabinet of Ministers' Scientific Advisory Committee and set up the Indian National Committee for Space Research. It was Dr. Bhabha who asked Dr. Vikram Sarabhai to take over the responsibility of the country's space research-related activities.

He died in a plane crash near Mont Blanc on January 24, 1966, while flying to Vienna, Austria, to represent India in the International Atomic Energy Agency's Scientific Advisory Committee. There were several allegations about this air crash including one of a conspiracy. The Government of India renamed the Atomic Energy Center in Trombay as Bhabha Atomic Research Center in honor of the pioneering legendary nuclear scientist.

As early as June 26, 1946, Pandit Jawaharlal Nehru, soon to be India's first Prime Minister, announced: "As long as the world is constituted as it is, every country will have to devise and use the latest devices for its protection. I have no doubt India will develop her scientific researches and I hope Indian scientists will use the atomic force for constructive purposes. But if India is threatened, she will inevitably try to defend herself by all means at her disposal."

Nuclear power is the fourth-largest source of electricity in India after thermal, hydro and renewable sources of electricity. As of 2008, India has 17 nuclear power plants in operation generating 4,120 MW while 6 other are under construction and are expected to generate an additional 3,160 MW. India is also involved in the development of fusion reactors through its participation in the ITER project.

Since early 1990s, Russia has been a major source of nuclear fuel to India. Due to dwindling domestic uranium reserves, electricity generation from nuclear power in India declined by 12.83% from 2006 to 2008. Following a waiver from the Nuclear Suppliers Group in September 2008 which allowed it to commence international nuclear trade, India has signed nuclear deals with several other countries including France, United States, and Kazakhstan while the framework for similar deals with Canada and United Kingdom are also being prepared. In February 2009, India also signed a $700 million deal with Russia for the supply of 2000 tons nuclear fuel.

India now envisages to increase the contribution of nuclear power to overall electricity generation capacity from 4.2% to 9% within 25 years. In 2010, India's installed nuclear power generation capacity will increase to 6,000 MW. As of 2009, India stands 9th in the world in terms of number of operational nuclear power reactors and is constructing 9 more, including two EPRs being constructed by France's Avera. Indigenous atomic reactors include TAPS-3, and -4, both of which are 540 MW reactors. India's $717 million fast breeder reactor project is expected to be operational by 2010.

Growth

India, being a non-signatory of the Nuclear Non-Proliferation Treaty, has been subjected to a defacto nuclear embargo from members of the Nuclear Suppliers Group (NSG) cartel. This has prevented India from obtaining commercial nuclear fuel, nuclear power plant components and services from the international market, thereby forcing India to develop its own fuel, components and services for nuclear power generation. The NSG embargo has had both negative and positive consequences for India's Nuclear Industry. On one hand, the NSG regime has constrained India from freely importing nuclear fuel at the volume and cost levels it would like to support the country's goals of expanding its nuclear power generation capacity to at least 20,000 MW by 2020. Also, by precluding India from taking advantage of the economies of scale and safety innovations of the global nuclear industry, the NSG regime has driven up the capital and operating costs and damaged the achievable safety potential of Indian nuclear power plants. On the other hand, the NSG embargo has forced the Indian government and bureaucracy to support and actively fund the development of Indian nuclear technologies and industrial capacities in all key areas required to create and maintain a domestic nuclear industry. This has resulted in the creation of a large pool of nuclear scientists, engineers and technicians that have developed new and unique innovations in the areas of Fast Breeder Reactors, Thermal Breeder Reactors, the Thorium fuel cycle, nuclear fuel reprocessing and Tritium extraction & production. Ironically, had the NSG sanctions not been in place, it would have been far more cost effective for India to import foreign nuclear power plants and nuclear fuels than to fund the development of Indian nuclear power generation technology, building of India's own nuclear reactors, and the development of domestic uranium mining, milling and refining capacity.

The Indian nuclear power industry is expected to undergo a significant expansion in the coming years thanks in part to the passing of The Indo-US nuclear deal. This agreement will allow India to carry out trade of nuclear fuel and technologies with other countries and significantly enhance its power generation capacity. When the agreement goes through, India is expected to generate an additional 25,000 MW of nuclear power by 2020, bringing total estimated nuclear power generation to 45,000 MW.

India has already been using imported enriched uranium and is currently under International Atomic Energy Agency (IAEA) safeguards, but it has developed various aspects of the nuclear fuel cycle to support its reactors. Development of select technologies has been strongly affected by limited imports. Use of heavy water reactors has been particularly attractive for the nation because it allows Uranium to be burnt with little to no enrichment capabilities. India has also done a great amount of work in the development of a Thorium centered fuel cycle. While Uranium deposits in the nation are limited (see next paragraph) there are much greater reserves of Thorium and it could provide hundreds of times the energy with the same mass of fuel. The fact that Thorium can theoretically be utilized in heavy water reactors has tied the development of the two. A prototype reactor that would burn Uranium-Plutonium fuel while irradiating a Thorium blanket is under construction at the Madras/Kalpakkam Atomic Power Station.

Uranium used for the weapons program has been separate from the power program, using Uranium from indigenous reserves. This domestic reserve of 80,000 to 112,000 tons of uranium (approx 1% of global uranium reserves) is large enough to supply all of India's commercial and military reactors as well as supply all the needs of India's nuclear weapons arsenal. Currently, India's nuclear power reactors consume, at most, 478 metric tonnes of uranium per year. Even if India were quadruple its nuclear power output (and reactor base) to 20GWe by 2020, nuclear power generation would only consume 2000 metric tonnes of uranium per annum. Based on India's known commercially viable reserves of 80,000 to 112,000 tons of uranium, this represents a 40 to 50 years uranium supply for India's nuclear power reactors (note with reprocessing and breeder reactor technology, this supply could be stretched out many times over). Furthermore, the uranium requirements of India's Nuclear Arsenal are only a fifteenth (1/15) of that required for power generation (approx. 32 tonnes), meaning that India's domestic fissile material supply is more than enough to meet all needs for it strategic nuclear arsenal. Therefore, India has sufficient uranium resources to meet its strategic and power requirements for the foreseeable future.

India possesses an arsenal of nuclear weapons and maintains short- range and intermediate-range ballistic missiles, nuclear-capable aircraft, surface ships, and submarines under development as possible delivery systems and platforms. Although it lacks an operational ballistic missile submarines India has ambitions of possessing a nuclear triad in the near future when INS Arihant the lead ship of India's Arihant class of nuclear-powered submarines formally joins the Indian Navy in 2012 after undergoing extensive sea-trials. Though India has not made any official statements about the size of its nuclear arsenal, estimates suggest that India has between 40 and 95 nuclear weapons, consistent with estimates that it has produced enough weapons-grade plutonium for up to 75-110 nuclear weapons. Production of weapons-grade plutonium production is believed to be taking place at the Bhabha Atomic Research Centre, which is home to the CIRUS reactor acquired from Canada, to the indigenous Dhruva reactor, and to a plutonium separation facility.

In November 2008, the Bulletin of the Atomic Scientists estimated that India has about 70 assembled nuclear warheads, with about 50 of them fully operational.

Former R&AW official J.K. Sinha, claimed that India has capability to produce 130 kilograms of weapon grade plutonium per year from six unsafeguarded reactors not included in the nuclear deal between India and the United States.

International Atomic Energy Agency (IAEA)

The International Atomic Energy Agency (IAEA) is an international organization that seeks to promote the peaceful use of nuclear energy and to inhibit its use for military purposes. It was established as an autonomous organization on 29 July 1957. Though established independently of the United Nations under its own international treaty (the IAEA Statute), the IAEA reports to both the General Assembly and the Security Council.

The IAEA has its headquarters in Vienna, Austria. Two "Regional Safeguards Offices" are located in Toronto, Canada; and Tokyo, Japan. The IAEA has two liaison offices, located in New York, USA; and Geneva, Switzerland. In addition, it has laboratories in Seibersdorf and Vienna, Austria; Monaco; and Trieste, Italy.

Today, the IAEA serves as an intergovernmental forum for scientific and technical co-operation in the peaceful use of nuclear technology worldwide. The IAEA's programs encourage the development of the peaceful applications of nuclear technology, provide international safeguards against its misuse and facilitate the application of safety measures in its use. The organization and its Director General, Mohamed ElBaradei, were jointly awarded the Nobel Peace Prize announced on 7 October 2005.

In 1953, U.S. President Dwight D. Eisenhower envisioned the creation of this international body to control and develop the use of atomic energy, in his *"Atoms for Peace"* speech before the UN General Assembly. In September 1954 the United States announced to the United Nations General Assembly a plan to create an international agency to take control of the fissile material being used to create nuclear reactors, establishing a kind of nuclear bank, and the United States called for an international scientific conference on all peaceful aspects of atomic energy. By November 1954 it was clear that the Soviets rejected actual international custody of fissile material, but that a *clearing house* for nuclear transactions might be possible. From 8 to 20 August 1955 the United Nations held the International Conference on the Peaceful Uses of Atomic Energy in Geneva. In 1956 an IAEA Statute Conference was held to draft foundation documents for the IAEA, and the IAEA Statute was completed at a 1957 conference.

In 1986, in response to the Chernobyl disaster, IAEA expanded its nuclear safety efforts.

The IAEA was headed by former Swedish Foreign Minister Hans Blix, who served as Director General from 1981 to 1997. The current Director General is the Egyptian Mohamed ElBaradei, who succeeded Blix and was approved by the 49th General Conference for a third term as Director General, through November 2009.

The Agency and Director General Mohamed ElBaradei were awarded the Nobel Peace Prize in 2005. In Dr. ElBaradei's speech he stated that only 1% of the money spent on developing new weapons would be enough to feed the entire world and that, if we hope to escape self-destruction, then nuclear weapons should have no place in our collective conscience, and no role in our security. Nobel Lecture.

On July 2, 2009, Yukiya Amano was elected as Director General for the IAEA, defeating Abdul Samad Minty of South Africa and Luis E. Echávarri of Spain. On 3 July 2009, the Board of Governors voted to appoint Yukiya Amano "by acclamation," and IAEA General Conference in September 2009 approved. He will take office on 1 December 2009.

Amano was born in Kanagawa Prefecture, Japan, in 1947. He started his studies at the Tokyo University in 1968. After graduating from the Faculty of Law, he joined the Ministry of Foreign Affairs in April 1972. He specialized in the international disarmament issue and nuclear nonproliferation efforts. In 1973–1974, he studied at the University of Franche-Comté and in 1974–1975, at the University of Nice, France.

Amano held different posts in the foreign ministry such as the Director of the Science Division and Director of the Nuclear Energy Division in 1993. During his foreign service, he was posted in the Embassies of Japan in Vientiane, Washington and Brussels, in the Delegation of Japan to the Conference on Disarmament in Geneva and was Consul General of Japan in Marseille.

In August 2002, he was appointed Director-General for Arms Control and Scientific Affairs, and in August 2004, he was appointed Director-General of the Disarmament, Nonproliferation and Science Department. Since 2005, he serves as the ambassador of Japan to the IAEA. From September 2005 to September 2006, Amano served as the Chairman of the IAEA Board of Governors. During his tenure, the IAEA and its Director General Mohamed ElBaradei received the Nobel Peace Prize. Amano represented the IAEA as the chairman at the Nobel Prize award ceremony held in December 2005.

In September 2008, the Japanese government announced that it nominated Yukiya Amano to the next Director General of the IAEA. On 2 July 2009, he was elected by the Board of Governors as Director General for the IAEA in the sixth round of voting defeating South African representative Abdul Samad Minty, his main rival. On 3 July 2009, all 145 IAEA member states will formally appoint Yukiya Amano "by acclamation" and he will be officially named after approving by simple majority of votes at the IAEA's General Conference in September 2009. He will begin his term on 30 November 2009.

In an interview to the Austrian newspaper *Die Presse*, Yukiya Amano said he was "resolute in opposing the spread of nuclear arms because I am from a country that experienced Hiroshima and Nagasaki".

The **Nuclear program of Iran** was launched in the 1950s with the help of the United States as part of the Atoms for Peace program. The support, encouragement and participation of the United States and Western European governments in Iran's nuclear program continued until the 1979 Islamic revolution that toppled the Shah of Iran.

After the Iranian Revolution in 1979, the Iranian government temporarily disbanded elements of the program, and then revived it with less Western assistance than during the pre-revolution era. Iran's nuclear program has included several research sites, a uranium mine, a nuclear reactor, and uranium processing facilities that include three known uranium enrichment plants.

Iran's first nuclear power plant, Bushehr, is expected to be operational in 2009. There are no current plans to complete the Bushehr II reactor, although the construction of 19 nuclear power plants is envisaged. Iran has announced that it is working on a new 360 MWe nuclear power plant to be located in Darkhovin. Iran has also indicated that it will seek more medium-sized nuclear power plants and uranium mines for the future.

The controversy over Iran's nuclear programs centers in particular on Iran's failure to declare sensitive enrichment and reprocessing activities to the IAEA. Enrichment can be used to produce uranium for reactor fuel or (at higher enrichment levels) for weapons. Iran says its nuclear program is peaceful, and has enriched uranium to less than 5 percent, consistent with fuel for a civilian nuclear power plant. Iran also claims that it was forced to resort to secrecy after US pressure caused several of its nuclear contracts with foreign governments to fall through. After the IAEA Board of Governors reported Iran's noncompliance with its safeguards agreement to the UN Security Council, the Council demanded that Iran suspend its nuclear enrichment activities while Iranian President Mahmoud Ahmadinejad has argued that the sanctions are "illegal," imposed by "arrogant powers," and that Iran has decided to pursue the monitoring of its self-described peaceful nuclear program through "its appropriate legal path," the International Atomic Energy Agency.

After public allegations about Iran's previously undeclared nuclear activities, the IAEA launched an investigation that concluded in November 2003 that Iran had systematically failed to meet its obligations under its NPT safeguards agreement to report those activities to the IAEA, although it also reported no evidence of links to a nuclear weapons program. The IAEA Board of Governors delayed a formal finding of non-compliance until September 2005, and (in a rare non-consensus decision) reported that non-compliance to the UN Security Council in February 2006. After the IAEA Board of Governors reported Iran's noncompliance with its safeguards agreement to the United Nations Security Council, the Council demanded that Iran suspend its enrichment programs. The Council imposed sanctions after Iran refused to do so. A May 2009 U.S. Congressional Report suggested "the United States, and later the Europeans, argued that Iran's deception meant it should forfeit its right to enrich, a position likely to be up for negotiation in talks with Iran. In exchange for suspending its enrichment program, Iran has been offered "a long-term comprehensive arrangement which would allow for the development of relations and cooperation with Iran based on mutual respect and the establishment of international confidence in the exclusively peaceful nature of Iran's nuclear program." However, Iran has consistently refused to give up its enrichment program, arguing that the program is necessary for its energy security, that such "long term arrangements" are inherently unreliable, and would deprive it of its inalienable right to peaceful nuclear technology. Currently, thirteen states possess operational enrichment or reprocessing facilities, and several others have expressed an interest in developing indigenous enrichment programs. Iran's position was endorsed by the Non-Aligned Movement, which expressed concern about the potential monopolization of nuclear fuel production.

To address concerns that its enrichment program may be diverted to non-peaceful uses, Iran has offered to place additional restrictions on its enrichment program including, for example, ratifying the Additional Protocol to allow more stringent inspections by the International Atomic Energy Agency, operating the uranium enrichment facility at Natanz as a multinational fuel center with the participation of foreign representatives, renouncing plutonium reprocessing and immediately fabricating all enriched uranium into reactor fuel rods. Iran's offer to open its uranium enrichment program to foreign private and public participation mirrors suggestions of an IAEA expert committee which was formed to investigate the methods to reduce the risk that sensitive fuel cycle activities could contribute to national nuclear weapons capabilities. Some non-governmental U.S. experts have endorsed this approach. The United States has insisted that Iran must meet the demands of the UN Security Council to suspend its enrichment program.

In every other case in which the IAEA Board of Governors made a finding of safeguards non-compliance involving clandestine enrichment or reprocessing, the resolution has involved (in the cases of Iraq and Libya) or is expected to involve (in the case of North Korea) at a minimum ending sensitive fuel cycle activities. According to Pierre Goldschmidt, former deputy director general and head of the department of safeguards at the IAEA, and Henry D. Sokolski, Executive Director of the Nonproliferation Policy Education Center, some other instances of safeguards noncompliance reported by the IAEA Secretariat (South Korea, Egypt) were never reported to the Security Council because the IAEA Board of Governors never made a formal finding of non-compliance. Though South Korea's case involved enriching uranium to levels near weapons grade, South Korea said it had voluntarily reported an isolated activity and Goldschmidt has argued "political considerations also played a dominant role in the board's decision" to not make a formal finding of non-compliance.

In January 1978, Kraftwerk Union stopped working at the Bushehr nuclear project with one reactor 50% complete, and the other reactor 85% complete, and fully withdrew from the project in July 1979. Iran paid Germany in full, totaling billions of dollars, for the two nuclear facilities in Bushehr. By July 1979, Iran had paid Kraftwerk Union $2.5 billion of the total contract.

When France after 1979 refused to give any enriched uranium to Iran and also Eurodif didn't return Iran's investments, Iran's government suspended its payments and tried to get refunded the loan by making pressure on France by handling militant groups, including the Hezbollah who took French citizens hostage in the 1980s.

Between March 24, 1984 to 1988, the Bushehr reactors were damaged by multiple Iraqi air strikes and work on the nuclear program came to a standstill. In January 1979, Kraftwerk Union (see 1970s) stopped working at the Bushehr nuclear project with one reactor 50% complete, and the other reactor 85% complete, and fully withdrew from the project in July 1979. Kraftwerk said they based their action on Iran's non-payment of $450 million in overdue payments. The company had then received $2.5 billion of the total contract. The French company Framatome, a subsidiary of Areva, also withdrew itself.

Another result of the 1979 Revolution was France's refusal to give any enriched uranium to Iran after 1979. Iran also didn't get back its investment from Eurodif. In 1982, French president François Mitterrand refused to give any uranium to Iran, which also claimed the $1 billion debt.

In 1984, Kraftwerk Union did a preliminary assessment to see if it could resume work on the project, but declined to do so while the Iran–Iraq War continued.

Timeline of nuclear program of Iran

IAEA reactions 1979-89

In 1983 the IAEA planned to provide assistance to Iran under its Technical Assistance Program to produce enriched uranium. An IAEA report stated that its aim was to "contribute to the formation of local expertise and manpower needed to sustain an ambitious program in the field of nuclear power reactor technology and fuel cycle technology".

U.S. reactions 1979-89

The United States in or after 1983 persuaded the IAEA to terminate its project to assist Iran in producing enriched uranium. In April 1984, the U.S. State Department said, "We believe it would take at least two to three years to complete construction of the reactors at Bushehr." The spokesperson also said that the light water power reactors at Bushehr "are not particularly well-suited for a weapons program." The spokesman went on to say, "In addition, we have no evidence of Iranian construction of other facilities that would be necessary to separate plutonium from spent reactor fuel."

Argentine refueling of research reactor 1987–93

According to a report by the Argentine justice in 2006, Iran in 1987–88 signed three agreements with Argentina's National Atomic Energy Commission. The first Iranian-Argentine agreement involved help in converting the U.S. supplied Tehran Nuclear Research Center (TNRC) research reactor from highly enriched uranium fuel to 19.75% low-enriched uranium, and to supply the low-enriched uranium to Iran. The uranium was delivered in 1993.The second and third agreements were for technical assistance, including components, for the building of pilot plants for uranium-dioxide conversion and fuel fabrication. Under US pressure, assistance under second and third agreements was reduced.

1993: China provides Iran with an HT-6B Tokamak fusion reactor that is installed at the Plasma Physics Research Centre of Azad University.

January 1995: Iran signs an $800 million contract with the Russian Ministry of Atomic Energy (MinAtom) to complete reactors at Bushehr under IAEA safeguards.

1996: China and Iran inform the IAEA of plans to construct a nuclear enrichment facility in Iran, but China withdraws from the contract under U.S. pressure. Iran advises the IAEA that it plans to pursue the construction anyway.

2002

January 29: U.S. president George W. Bush speaks of an "Axis of evil" gathering Iran, Iraq and North Korea during his State of the Union Address.

August: The exiled opposition National Council of Resistance of Iran reports the existence of an uranium enrichment facility at Natanz and a heavy water plant at Arak.

December: The United States accuses Iran of an "across-the-board pursuit of weapons of mass destruction".

2003

February: International Atomic Energy Agency (IAEA) inspects the Natanz and Arak facilities.

June: An IAEA report on the inspections says that Iran has failed to comply with the nuclear Non-Proliferation Treaty.

September 12: The International Atomic Energy Agency gives Iran a deadline to reveal all the details of its nuclear activities by October 31, 2003.

September 30: International Atomic Energy Agency Director General Mohamed ElBaradei and a team of inspectors begin a visit to Iran to begin talks and inspections.

November 11: The IAEA reports that Iran had many breaches and failures to comply with its safeguards agreement, including a "policy of concealment" from the IAEA, but also states that there is "no evidence" that Iran is attempting to build an atomic bomb.

November 13: The Bush administration claims that the IAEA conclusion of "no evidence" is "impossible to believe."

December 18, 2003: As agreed in the Paris Agreement, Iran voluntarily signs and implements the Additional Protocol to the Nuclear Non-Proliferation Treaty Though the Protocol was not binding on Iran until ratified, Iran voluntarily agrees to permit expanded and more intensive IAEA inspections pursuant to the Protocol, which fail to turn up a nuclear weapons program in Iran. Iran ends the voluntarily implementation of Additional Protocol after two years of inspections, as a protest to continued EU-3 demands that Iran abandon all enrichment.

2004

June 14: Mohamed ElBaradei, Director General of the International Atomic Energy Agency, accuses Iran of "less than satisfactory" co-operation during the IAEA investigation of its nuclear program. ElBaradei demands "accelerated and proactive cooperation" from Iran which exceed the terms of Iran's legal obligations.

June 29: IAEA Director General Mohammad El-Baradei announced that the Bushehr reactor was "not of international concern" since it was a bilateral Russian-Iranian project intended to produce nuclear energy.

July 27: Iran removes seals placed upon uranium centrifuges by the International Atomic Energy Agency and resumes construction of the centrifuges at Natanz.

August 10: Several long-standing charges and questions regarding weapons-grade uranium samples found in Iran are clarified by the IAEA. Some samples match Pakistani and Russian sources which had contaminated imported Iranian equipment from those countries. The sources of the remaining samples remain unaccounted for.

November 15: Talks between Iran and three European Union members, the United Kingdom, France, and Germany, result in a compromise. Iran agrees to temporarily suspend its active uranium enrichment program for the duration of a second round of talks, during which attempts will be made at arriving at a permanent, mutually-beneficial solution.

November 15: A confidential UN report is leaked. The report states that all nuclear materials within Iran have been accounted for and there is no evidence of any military nuclear program. Nevertheless, it still cannot discount the possibility of such a program because it does not have perfect knowledge.

November 22: Iran declares that it will voluntarily suspend its uranium enrichment program to enter negotiations with the EU. Iran will review its decision in three months. The EU seeks to have the suspension made permanent and is willing to provide economic and political incentives.

November 24: Iran seeks to obtain permission from the European Union, in accordance with its recent agreement with the EU, to allow it to continue working with 24 centrifuges for research purposes.

2005

June 2005: U.S. Secretary of State Condoleezza Rice said IAEA head Mohamed ElBaradei should either "toughen his stance on Iran" or fail to be chosen for a third term as the agency's head. Following a one on one meeting between Rice and ElBaradei on June 9, the United States withdrew its opposition and ElBaradei was re-elected to his position on June 13, 2005.

Between August 8 and August 10: Iran resumed the conversion of uranium at the Isfahan facility, under IAEA safeguards, but did not engage in enrichment of uranium.

August 9: The Iranian Head of State, Ayatollah Ali Khamenei, issued a fatwa forbidding the production, stockpiling and use of nuclear weapons. The full text of the fatwa was released in an official statement at the meeting of the International Atomic Energy Agency in Vienna.

August 10: Iran begins to remove International Atomic Energy Agency seals at the Uranium Conversion Facility in Esfahan.

August 11: The 35-member governing board of the IAEA adopted a resolution calling upon Iran to suspend uranium conversion, and instructing ElBaradei to submit a report on Iran's nuclear program by September 3, 2005.

August 15: Iran's new president, Mahmoud Ahmadinejad, installed his new government. Iranian presidents do not have exclusive control over Iran's nuclear program, which falls mainly under the purview of Iran's Supreme Leader. Ali Larijani replaced Hassan Rowhani as secretary of the Supreme National Security Council, Iran's top policy-making body, with nuclear policy in his purview.

September 2: IAEA report says that Iran has resumed uranium conversion at the Isfahan nuclear research facility.

November 5: The Iranian government approved a plan that allows foreign investors to participate in the work at the Natanz uranium enrichment plant. The cabinet also authorized the AEOI to take necessary measures to attract foreign and domestic investment in the uranium enrichment process.

2006

January 10: Iran resumes nuclear fuel research at the Natanz enrichment plant after breaking the UN seals on the facility.

January 31: The IAEA reports that "Iran has continued to facilitate access under its Safeguards Agreement as requested by the Agency ... including by providing in a timely manner the requisite declarations and access to locations" and lists outstanding issues.

February 4: The IAEA votes 27-3 to report Iran to the United Nations Security Council. After the vote, Iran announced its intention to end voluntary co-operation with the IAEA beyond basic Nuclear Non-Proliferation Treaty requirements, and to resume enrichment of uranium.

February 5: Iran ends snap UN nuclear inspections.

February 14: Iran restarts small-scale feeding of uranium gas into centrifuges at Natanz after a two-and-a-half year suspension.

February 16: French Foreign Minister Philippe Douste-Blazy said "No civilian nuclear program can explain the Iranian nuclear program. It is a clandestine military nuclear program."

April 11: Iran announces it has produced low-grade enriched uranium suitable for use in power stations, a move confirmed by the IAEA.

April 26: Supreme Leader of Iran, Ayatollah Ali Khamenei said that Americans should know that if they assault Iran their interests will be harmed anywhere in the world that is possible, and that the Iranian nation will respond to any blow with double the intensity.

May 12: AP published an interview with Pakistan's former chief of staff of the Pakistan Army Mirza Aslam Beg in the AP interview; Beg detailed nearly 20 years of Iranian approaches to obtain conventional arms and then technology for nuclear weapons. He described an Iranian visit in 1990, when he was army chief of staff.

They didn't want the technology. They asked: 'Can we have a bomb?' My answer was: By all means you can have it but you must make it yourself. Nobody gave it to us.

Beg said he is sure Iran has had enough time to develop them. But he insists the Pakistani government didn't help, even though he says former Prime Minister Benazir Bhutto once told him the Iranians offered more than $4 billion for the technology.

June 5: Javier Solana, European Union foreign policy chief, delivers a package of incentives from world powers if Iran agrees to halt uranium enrichment.

August 31: The IAEA announces Iran has not met a deadline to suspend its atomic fuel program.

September 16: (Havana, Cuba) All of the 118 Non-Aligned Movement member countries declare their support for Iran's nuclear program for civilian purposes in their final written statement. That is a clear majority of the 192 countries comprising the entire United Nations.

December 23: Security Council votes for sanctions and gives Iran a 60-day deadline to suspend enrichment. Iran calls the resolution illegal.

2007

January 2007: former French President Jacques Chirac, speaking "off the record" to reporters from The New York Times, indicated that if Iran possessed a nuclear weapon, the weapon could not be used. Chirac alluded to mutually assured destruction when he stated: "Where will it drop it, this bomb? On Israel? It would not have gone 200 meters into the atmosphere before Tehran would be razed."

January 15: Ardeshir Hosseinpour, an Iranian junior scientist involved in The Uranium Conversion Facility at Isfahan, dies, reportedly due to "gassing". Several other scientists may also be killed or injured, and treated in nearby hospitals.

January 21: The death of Ardeshir Hosseinpour is finally reported by the Al-Quds daily and the Iranian Student's News Agency (in Arabic & Persian).

February 2: The U.S. private intelligence company Stratfor releases a report saying that Ardeshir Hosseinpour was killed by the Mossad through radioactive poisoning.

March 24: The Security Council unanimously approves further financial and weapons sanctions against Iran.

April 9: President Ahmadinejad has announced Iran can now produce nuclear fuel on an industrial scale. Some officials said 3,000 uranium gas enrichment centrifuges were running at the Natanz plant in central Iran.

April 18: The IAEA says Iran has begun making nuclear fuel in an underground uranium enrichment plant.

May 23: A confidential IAEA report says Iran has not suspended enrichment-related work.

August 21: Iran and the IAEA say they have agreed a timeline for answering the watchdog's outstanding questions about Iran's nuclear program.

October 16: Vladimir Putin visited Tehran, Iran to participate in the Second Caspian Summit, where he met with Iranian leader Mahmoud Ahmadinejad. At a press conference after the summit Putin said that "Iran has the right to develop their peaceful nuclear programs without any restrictions".

October 20: Saeed Jalili is named as Iran's new chief nuclear negotiator. He replaces Ali Larijani, who resigned.

October 24: The US imposes new sanctions on Iran and accuses the elite Revolutionary Guard of spreading weapons of mass destruction.

November 2: Britain, France, Germany, the US, Russia and China (the group of six) agree to push ahead with a third round of tougher sanctions.

November 15: The IAEA says Iran has made important strides towards transparency but it remains unable to ascertain whether Iran has a secret, parallel military enrichment program.

November 30: The EU expresses disappointment with Iran after more talks with its main nuclear negotiator in London.

December 1: A meeting of world powers in Paris fails to reach an agreement on further sanctions.

December 3: A US National Intelligence Estimate says Iran halted its attempts to build a nuclear bomb in 2003.

December 5: Victory over the US is declared by Ahmadinejad.

December 11: Opposition coalition NCRI says that Iran's program was shut down in 2003 and re-started a year later, adding that the recent US analysis was misleading.

2008

March 4: The UN Security Council adopts Resolution 1803 - the third sanction resolution on Iran with a 14-0 vote (Indonesia abstained). The resolution extends financial sanctions to additional banks, extends travel bans to additional persons and bars exports to Iran of nuclear and missile-related dual-use items.

March 24: The last shipment of fuel and equipment arrives at the Bushehr Nuclear Power Plant.

May 14: Russia's foreign minister says an offer to negotiate and security guarantees for Iran could be given by the group of six. The US administration denies that security guarantees were being considered.

May 26: The IAEA says Iran's alleged research into nuclear warheads is a matter of serious concern and asks for more information on Tehran's missile-related activities.

June 1: In reaction to the IAEA's report, Tehran says it might have to limit cooperation with them.

June 14: Solana, in Tehran, presents Iran with an offer from world powers with economic and other benefits. However, Iran rejects any suspension of activities.

July 10: Iran tests nine missiles in the Gulf.

July 19: Iranian officials rule out freeze in uranium enrichment during talks in Geneva, attended for the first time by a senior US diplomat.

August 2: An informal deadline lapses for Iran to respond to an offer from the United States, Britain, France, Germany, China and Russia for talks.

September 15: The IAEA says Iran blocks a UN inquiry into whether it researched ways to develop a nuclear bomb.

2009

February 5: Russia says it plans to start up a nuclear reactor at the Bushehr plant by the end of 2009.

February 19: An IAEA report shows a significant increase in Iran's stockpile of low-enriched uranium; enough, physicists say, for conversion into highly enriched uranium for one bomb.

March 20: Barack Obama, as the new US president, calls for "engagement that is honest and grounded in mutual respect" with Iran.

Iran cautiously welcomes the overture, but said it wanted to see "practical steps".

April 9: Ahmadinejad says Iran has mastered the nuclear fuel cycle and also tested further advanced machines for enriching uranium. President also inaugurates the nation's first atomic fuel fabrication plant near Isfahan.

June 5: A quarterly IAEA report says Iran now has 7,231 centrifuge enrichment machines installed, a 25 per cent increase in potential capacity since March.

June 12: Ahmadinejad re-elected president. Protests break out by moderates who say the result was fixed.

July 5: US Vice President Joseph Biden stated in an interview with ABC News that the United States would not stop an Israeli attack on Iran: "If the Netanyahu government decides to take a course of action different than the one being pursued now, that is their sovereign right to do that. That is not our choice." When Israeli Prime Minister Benjamin Netanyahu was in United States, spring 2009, he said that he had agreed to give President Barack Obama's engagement policy until the end of the year to "bear some fruit." After that deadline passed, Israel would feel free to take on the "existential threat" posed by Iran with military force if necessary.

August 21: Iran allows IAEA officials to inspect the Arak heavy-water site as well as an upgrade to IAEA monitoring at the Natanz uranium enrichment plant. Diplomats say there has been no increase in the number of centrifuges enriching uranium since the end of May.

August 28: The IAEA reports Iran has slightly reduced the scale of its uranium enrichment. But it has also raised the number of installed centrifuge machines by some 1,000 to 8,308.

August 28: The United Arab Emirates seized a North Korean ship secretly carrying embargoed North Korean arms to Iran. Among the weapons in the ship, were rocket-propelled grenades.

September 7: Ahmadinejad says Iran will continue its disputed nuclear work and will never negotiate on its "obvious" rights.

September 9: Iran hands over a package of proposals to six world powers - the US, Russia, China, France, Britain and Germany -

which it says addresses "various global issues" and represents a "new opportunity for talks and cooperation".

September 17: Ahmadinejad says Iran would "never" abandon its nuclear program to appease Western critics.

September 25: The IAEA says Iran has told it about a second uranium enrichment plant under construction. Obama announces that the US, UK and France provided evidence to the IAEA showing Iran has been developing a covert uranium enrichment facility near Qom for several years.

September 26: Ahmadinejad reacts strongly to international condemnation of the second uranium enrichment facility, saying it was within the "parameters of the UN nuclear watchdog's rules".

September 27: Hillary Clinton, the US secretary of state, welcomes Iran's decision to allow IAEA inspectors into a newly disclosed uranium enrichment plant.

September 29: Iran test-fires several ballistic missiles.

September 30: Iran says it will not negotiate over its right to develop a nuclear program when it meets officials from the five permanent members of the UN Security Council and Germany in Geneva on October 1.

October 1: Iran meets six world powers in Geneva. Saeed Jalili, Iran's chief nuclear negotiator holds talks with William Burns, a senior US official in Geneva, in the most high-level US-Iranian contact in three decades.

October 3: The New York Times reports that staff at the International Atomic Energy Agency have written a confidential analysis conveying that Iran has "sufficient information to be able to design and produce a workable" atom bomb.

October 4: The IAEA announces that its inspectors will examine the Qom plant on October 25.

October19: An Iranian official says Tehran will not abandon its uranium enrichment activities, regardless of the outcome of talks with world powers.

October20: France said that talks on Iran's nuclear program were continuing in Vienna, despite Tehran's assertion that French participation is unnecessary.

Day two of international talks in Vienna on Iran's nuclear program was stalled after Iran indicated that it did not want French participation in negotiations on a proposal to have Iran ship uranium to Russia and France for conversion to reactor fuel.

October 21: The IAEA says Iran has agreed to consider a deal which could see it ship out most of its enriched uranium to Russia.

October 22: A senior Iranian member of parliament rejects the idea of sending enriched uranium abroad for further processing, hinting at Tehran's reluctance to accept a proposal meant to ease tensions over its nuclear ambitions.

October 23: Iran fails to meet the deadline to accept the IAEA deal.

October24: The Obama administration signaled impatience with Iran after the Tehran government ignored a Friday deadline to respond to a U.N.-brokered deal aimed at easing concerns over its nuclear program. Iran has promised a reply by next week.

U.S. officials say they're willing to wait a few more days for an Iranian response to the nuclear proposals, but they say the Obama administration is looking for concrete action and does not have unlimited patience.

October25: U.N. nuclear experts inspect the newly disclosed centrifuge plant being built near the Shi'ite holy city of Qom. The site will refine uranium for civilian nuclear energy.

October26: Manouchehr Mottaki reportedly said Tehran may agree to ship some of its own uranium abroad for enriching, or it may choose to buy enriched uranium.

October27: Iran's state television says the country will accept the general framework of a United Nations-brokered uranium deal, but will demand some "important changes."

The network reported the development Tuesday saying the comments were made by unnamed officials with ties to Iran's nuclear negotiating team. The network also says Iran will offer its formal response to the U.N.-proposal "within 48 hours."

October28: A key congressional committee has approved legislation to expand sanctions against Iran because of its nuclear ambitions. The Iran Refined Petroleum Sanctions Act is aimed at placing additional pressure on Iran by punishing companies involved in assisting Iran's petroleum sector and gasoline imports.

October 29: Iran proposes changes to a U.N.-drafted atomic fuel deal, according to Iranian media, making demands that appeared to challenge the basis of the agreement with the United States, France and Russia.

October 29: The U.S. Senate Banking Committee has voted to approve legislation that would impose sanctions on companies that help Iran acquire refined petroleum products.

October30: Iran's powerful parliament speaker Ali Larijani attacked the United States Friday, accusing it of involvement in a recent bloody attack in Sistan-Baluchistan, which killed a number of top Revolutionary Guard commanders.

October31: Decision-makers gave thumbs down to the U.N. draft nuclear deal with the West, saying that they reject it in its current form. Several key members of parliament have slammed the deal, while President Mahmoud Ahmedinejad expressed displeasure with it, but urged the West to "continue cooperating with Iran."

November2: US Secretary of State Hillary Rodham Clinton said Monday that the nuclear offer to Iran, intended to restrain its potential for making a nuclear weapon, should be fully accepted by Iran and will not be changed.

"This is a pivotal moment for Iran," she said at a news conference after consulting with senior government officials from several Persian Gulf nations, plus Egypt, Morocco and Jordan.

November2: Iran said Monday it has not rejected an UN-backed plan aimed at limiting the country's ability to make nuclear weapons as it called for a technical panel to review its terms.

Foreign Minister Manouchehr Mottaki told reporters in Kuala Lumpur that Iran conveyed its stand to the International Atomic

Energy Agency two days ago. Mottaki is in Malaysia to attend a meeting of foreign ministers of eight Islamic countries.

November3: "The American government is a really arrogant power and the Iranian nation will not be deceived with its apparent reconciliatory behavior until America abandons its arrogant attitude," Khamenei was quoted as saying by state radio.

November3: In a speech to US Congress marking the 20th anniversary of the fall of the Berlin Wall, Merkel said that allowing Iran to have nuclear weapons, especially with a leader that denies the Holocaust, is "non-negotiable."

"A nuclear bomb in the hands of an Iranian president who denies the Holocaust, threatens Israel and denies Israel the right to exist is not acceptable," she said.

November3: Military Intelligence chief Maj.-Gen. Amos Yadlin said that the Israeli intelligence assessment is that Iran was interested in a "horizontal expansion" of its nuclear production capacity, so that when Tehran decides to advance to nuclear weapons capability, it will be able to do so in the shortest possible period of time.

Speaking at a briefing of the Knesset's Foreign Affairs and Defense Committee, Yadlin said that the Qom facility was designed for the enrichment of uranium, and at full capacity can hold 3,000 advanced centrifuges. "Iran isn't North Korea," he said.

November3: Hundreds of tons of weaponry, ten times the size of the Karine A shipment of 2002, were seized in an overnight raid by the Israeli navy, some 100 nautical miles west of Israel, officials said. The ship seized was sailing under an Antiguan flag. This is the largest arms seizure in Israel's history.

Defense officials said the 140-meter long Francop, captured near Cyprus, was carrying arms sent by Iran and destined for Syria and Hizbullah.

The weapons included 107-millimeter rockets, 60-millimeter mortars, 7.62-rifle Kalashnikov-ammunition, F-1 grenades and 122-millimeter Katyusha rockets. On the side of some of the cases inside the containers the words "parts of bulldozers" was written.

November4: US President Barack Obama noted Wednesday's 30th anniversary of the takeover of the US Embassy in Tehran, while insisting he wants the United States and Iran to move beyond the "path of sustained suspicion, mistrust and confrontation" that followed the subsequent hostage crisis.

The crisis "deeply affected the lives of courageous Americans who were unjustly held hostage, and we owe these Americans and their families our gratitude for their extraordinary service and sacrifice," Obama said.

November5: Prime Minister Benjamin Netanyahu said Thursday that the ship carrying hundreds of tons of weapons believed to have originated in Iran and meant for Hezbollah, which Israel intercepted early Wednesday, constituted a war crime that should be reviewed by United Nations bodies.

"The UN General Assembly should have investigated and condemned this crime and the UN Security Council should have convened a special session to debate this incident," Netanyahu continued._"This is a war crime which Iran intends to commit again in the future. The international community should be focusing on this, but instead, the world condemns Israel and the Israel Defense Forces and undermines our right to self defense." he said.

November5: The International Atomic Energy Agency has demanded that Iran explain evidence that it has experimented with advanced nuclear warhead technology, The Guardian reported. According to the report, the technology, called "two-point implosion," is considered to be a secret in the US as well as the UK. It allows development of smaller, simpler warheads, which are easier to place on missiles than older designs.

IAEA chief Mohamed ElBaradei said inspectors from the UN nuclear watchdog found "nothing to be worried about" at Iran's recently-revealed uranium enrichment site at Qom. An unnamed European advisor on nuclear issues told the newspaper: "It is breathtaking that Iran could be working on this sort of material."

November6: Israel is not bluffing when it warns that all options are still on the table and that it may strike Iranian nuclear facilities, Deputy Foreign Minister Danny Ayalon said in an interview with the British Sky television channel.

"The one who's bluffing is Iran, which is trying to play with cards they don't have," Ayalon reportedly said. "If Iranian behavior and conduct continues as they have exhibited so far, it is obvious that their intentions are only to buy time and procrastinate," Ayalon said.

November6: The IDF on Friday published new video clips documenting the moments when Navy commandos from the elite Flottila 13 unit raided the Francop cargo vessel, opened containers on board the ship and discovered a huge stash of armaments sent by Iran and bound for Syria, possibly intended for use by Hizbullah.

In the first moments of the operation, when the commandos did not know whether the crew would cooperate with the inspection of its cargo, they searched the vessel with weapons loaded and with bullets lodged in the barrel carrier.

The final weight of the cache was 320 tons and included 9,000 mortar shells, thousands of 107-mm. Katyusha rockets that have a range of 15 kilometers, some 600 Russian-made 122-mm. rockets with a 40-km. range and hundreds of thousands of Kalashnikov bullets.

November6: David Miliband, the British foreign minister, has said that the lack of a response from Tehran is "very disappointing".

"We haven't had a proper answer on that and it's disappointing to get that sort of engagement," he said in an interview to Al Jazeera."The international community has shown it does not seek to victimise Tehran. Tehran is the author of its own isolation."

November7: Iranian Students News Agency is featuring a comment by the head of Parliament's National Security and Foreign Policy Commission, Alaeddin Boroujerdi, "Iran is not to give any of its 1200 kilograms fuel to the other party to receive 20 percent (enriched) fuel and whether gradually or at once, this will not be done and is called off." Boroujerdi insisted that Iran must and would find another way to get uranium.

November8: A senior Iranian lawmaker warned Russia that its delay in delivering an anti-aircraft missile defense system to Tehran could harm relations between the two countries. Russia signed a contract two years ago to sell the S-300 surface-to-air missiles to Iran.

In 2007, Russia delivered Iran another anti-aircraft system called the Tor-M1, which can hit aerial targets at up to 20,000 feet.

November8: The Obama administration, attempting to salvage a faltering nuclear deal with Iran, has told Iran's leaders in back-channel messages that it is willing to allow the country to send its stockpile of enriched uranium to any of several nations, including Turkey, for temporary safekeeping, according to administration officials and diplomats involved in the exchanges.

But the overtures, made through the International Atomic Energy Agency over the past two weeks, have all been ignored, the officials said. Instead, they said, the Iranians have revived an old counter-proposal: that international arms inspectors take custody of much of Iran's fuel, but keep it on Kish, a Persian Gulf resort island that is part of Iran.

November9: The Iranian top nuclear negotiator, Saeed Jalili, said that Tehran "welcomes" talks on the nuclear issue with the five permanent UN Security Council members plus Germany. Jalili spoke during a meeting with visiting Russian deputy foreign minister, Sergei Ryabkov, according to Iran's state television.

November9: President Barack Obama said that an unsettled political situation in Iran may be complicating efforts to seal a nuclear fuel deal between Tehran and major world powers.

"But it is going to take time, and part of the challenge that we face is that neither North Korea nor Iran seem to be settled enough politically to make quick decisions on these issues," he said at the White House.

"Although so far we have not seen the kind of positive response we want from Iran, we are as well positioned as we've ever been to align the international community behind that agenda," Obama said.

November9: Foreign Minister Avigdor Lieberman compared Iran's regime with the Nazis when he spoke Monday in Copenhagen at a special ceremony in memory of the Danish Jews who were sent to the Theresienstadt concentration camp during World War II.

"The fight against the Iranian threat is one of the greatest challenges the democratic world faces today," he said.

November10: Iran is both "extreme" and "irrational," IDF Chief of General Staff Lt.-Gen. Gabi Ashkenazi told the Knesset Foreign Affairs and Defense Committee on Tuesday morning.

"There's a battle in the Middle East, between the radicals and the moderates," the IDF chief said, "which is pushing Iran to radical acts, to fund terror."

Meanwhile, Turkish and Iranian officials met secretly this week on the sidelines of an Istanbul summit, according to a Turkish daily.

November10: Iranian President Mahmoud Ahmadinejad called on the US to choose between Israel and Iran on Tuesday night, according to an Army Radio Report. He reportedly said that for a real change in relations to take place, a choice must be made.

Speaking in Istanbul, the Iranian president said that it was up to US President Barack Obama to illustrate his motto of "Change."

"The support of both Israel and Iran can't go hand in hand," he was quoted as saying.

November10: Iran plans to install 50,000 centrifuges to enrich uranium at its Natanz site and a recently disclosed facility near

Qom, Ahmadinejad said, to be used in as yet unbuilt power plants.

"Wherever we go beyond our needs, the surplus will be exported," the president added, speaking through an interpreter.

November10: "There needs to be a voice against destruction and against terror, a clear voice. I know that Brazil rejects threats, destruction, rejects terror, and the clear voice of Brazil has a strong echo in the entire world," Shimon Peres said in a speech before Brazilian lawmakers.

While Israel did not see the Iranian people as an enemy, "we cannot ignore that this government (of Ahmadinejad) is building nuclear weapons and at the same time calls for the destruction of the state of Israel," he added.

November11: Iran's defense minister urged Russia to ignore Israeli pressure against selling the S-300 missile defense system to the Islamic Republic.

"We have a contract with Russia to buy S-300 missiles. I don't think it is right for Russia to be seen in the world as a country which does not fulfill its contractual obligations," AFP quoted Iranian Defense Minister Vahidi as telling the ILNA news agency.

November11: "One of the most important issues of today is definitely nuclear cooperation at the international level, whether in building a power station or reactor or whether it is about Iran's presence in the global fuel bank," Ahmadinejad said. He declared Iran's readiness for international nuclear cooperation, including on a global fuel bank. Ahmadinejad said the issue of stopping Iran's nuclear activities was "finished," IRIB reported on its website. "Those people who yesterday told us that we should suspend our activities ... (today) they cannot say anything," he said, adding Iran would protect its "big nuclear achievements" with determination.

November12: One of the diplomats - a senior official from a European nation - said Thursday that the enrichment facility was too small to house the tens of thousands of centrifuges needed for peaceful industrial nuclear enrichment, but is the right size to contain the few thousand advanced machines that could generate the amount of weapons-grade uranium needed to make nuclear warheads.

The pauses in construction may reflect Tehran's determination to keep its activities secret as far back as 2002, when Iran's clandestine nuclear program was revealed. Citing satellite imagery, the diplomats said Iran started building the plant in 2002, paused for two years in 2004 - the same year it suspended enrichment on an international demand - and resumed construction in 2006, when enrichment was also restarted.

November13: French President Nicolas Sarkozy warned Syrian President Bashar Assad that Israel may strike Iranian nuclear facilities if an agreement on Tehran's nuclear program is not reached soon, London-based Al Hayat reported on Saturday.

November13: Iranian Chief of Staff Hassan Firouzabadi urged Russia to ship the S-300 surface-air missile system to Tehran in accordance with a contract signed between the two countries months ago, PressTV reported. According to the report, Firouzabadi expressed confusion over Moscow's six-month delay. "Don't Russian strategists realize Iran's geopolitical importance to their security?" the general was quoted as saying.

November13: Turkish Energy Minister Taner Yildiz said on Friday that if asked, his country would be willing to temporarily store

Iran's enriched uranium to help defuse a standoff over Western suspicions that Tehran is trying to build an atomic bomb.

Yildiz stated that storing low-level enriched uranium in Turkey would not pose a problem, adding that although such a request had not been made, the issue was still being discussed. If asked, he concluded, "we would not say no."

November14: The Russian leader has already expressed a willingness to consider further sanctions. In an interview last week with German newspaper *Der Spiegel* which was translated by Reuters, Medvedev said that "We wouldn't want this to end with international sanctions because sanctions, as a rule, take us in a very complex and dangerous direction. But if there is no movement forward, nobody is ruling out such a scenario." The newspaper quoted sources in the administration of Russian President Dmitry Medvedev as saying that Moscow was "100 percent ready" to back new sanctions.

November14: Iran has completely rejected an UN-brokered nuclear deal, but US President Barack Obama has postponed the official announcement on Tehran's refusal due to internal political reasons, Israel Radio quoted a senior western official as saying Saturday.

November15: On the sidelines of an Asia-Pacific meeting in Singapore, U.S. President Barack Obama said time was running out for diplomacy to resolve a crisis over Iran's nuclear program, but Russian President Dmitry Medvedev offered softer criticism of Tehran. "Unfortunately, so far at least, Iran appears to have been unable to say yes to what everyone acknowledges is a creative and constructive approach," Obama said while seated next to Medvedev. "We are running out of time with respect to that approach."

Repeating previous Russian language, Medvedev said "other means" could be used if discussions did not yield results, but did not specify what they might be. "Thanks to joint efforts the process of the Iran talks has not stopped but we are not completely happy about its pace. If something does not work there are other means to move the process further," he said. "Our aim is clear -- a transparent nuclear program rather than a program which causes others' concern."

November15: Iran will soon be able to produce an advanced missile defense system itself if Russia does not deliver it to the Islamic Republic, a senior lawmaker said in comments published on Sunday. The commander of Iran's air force, Brigadier General Hassan Shahsafi, separately announced plans to produce new "heat-seeking air-to-air missiles", Jomhuri Eslami newspaper reported.

November15: A former Iranian defense official who disappeared in 2007 was kidnapped by forces collaborating with the Mossad and is currently being held in an Israeli prison, an investigative news website in Iran claimed on Sunday in a report picked up by Army Radio. Ali-Reza Asgari, a onetime commander of Iran's Revolutionary Guard, went missing in Turkey in 2007.

The report claims that Asgari was kidnapped in an effort to get information about Iran's nuclear program and about missing Israel Air Force navigator Ron Arad. The report added that after his questioning, Asgari was secretly transferred to a prison facility in Israel, where he is currently being held.

November16: Iranian President Mahmoud Ahmadinejad on Monday reiterated that his country's rights on "the nuclear issue" are non-negotiable and its nuclear activities and cooperation happen within the framework of IAEA regulations, according to a report on the Iranian student news agency ISNA.

"Iran is ready for constructive and honest cooperation with western countries in the field of nuclear technology," he was quoted by ISNA as saying, while warning that the West's confrontation with Iran only makes the country "more powerful and more developed."

November16: Iran's belated revelation of a second uranium enrichment site raises concern about possible further secret nuclear sites in the country, according to a U.N. nuclear watchdog report on Monday obtained by Reuters.

It said Iran had told the International Atomic Energy Agency that it had begun building the bunkered site near Qom in 2007 but the IAEA had evidence the project began in 2002, paused in 2004 and resumed in 2006. Iran reported the site's existence to the IAEA in September.

The IAEA's report states "The agency has indicated (to Iran) that its declaration of the new facility reduces the level of confidence in the absence of other nuclear facilities under construction and gives rise to questions about whether there were any other nuclear facilities not declared to the agency. Moreover, Iran's delay in submitting such information to the agency does not contribute to the building of confidence." The IAEA also said Iran had yet to give answers about the site's chronology and purpose.

November16: US Senator Joe Lieberman said that Iran "has failed the test" in rejecting the hand extended by the United States and the international community. Today, one can say that Iran completely failed the test, and the ball is in Tehran's court, Senator Lieberman said at a joint press conference with a delegation of senators attending the Saban Forum parley in Jerusalem.

My conclusion is that the open hand extended to Iran by the United States and the international community has been met with a closed fist, the senator stated. The senator went on to say that today, it is clearer than ever that the Iranian government will not halt its nuclear program unless it is aware that the regime is in danger.

November 16: Iranian President Mahmoud Ahmadinejad carries the mark of Cain, President Shimon Peres said Monday at a luncheon hosted in his honor by Argentine President Cristina Kirchner. "We want to live in a civilized world in which a military man is not a killer," he continued, referring to Iran's defense minister Ahmad Wahidi who is known to be one of the key figures behind the bombings that claimed tens of lives and left hundreds wounded and maimed.

Peres praised Argentina for speaking out against Ahmadinejad who denies the Holocaust and calls for Israel's destruction and lauded Kirchner as "one of the outstanding leaders against racism and anti-Semitism." Kirchner said that her government absolutely condemned any form of racism or anti-Semitism, and could find no valid reason, religious or otherwise for one person to kill another.

November 17: A secret deal being drafted by outgoing International Atomic Energy Agency (IAEA) chief Mohamed ElBaradei would see Iran retain its nuclear program, as well as the removal of all sanctions placed on the Islamic Republic, simply in exchange for its cooperation with UN inspectors, The Times of London reported Tuesday.

Drafted in September, the document would allow Iran to keep and even to expand its uranium enrichment program, although under close inspection. If Iran met these terms, it would be relieved of the three rounds of sanctions placed on it by the UN

Security Council, as well as five resolutions demanding that it halt enrichment. The IAEA denied the document's existence, but a copy of it was obtained by The Times - reportedly leaked by a source that found its contents alarming.

November 17: China and the United States agree Iran must show its nuclear program is peaceful and transparent, President Barack Obama said on Tuesday, but Chinese President Hu Jintao was more guarded on the dispute at a summit in Beijing.

"We agreed that the Islamic Republic of Iran must provide assurance to the international community that its nuclear program is peaceful and transparent," Obama said at a news conference with Hu. "Iran has an opportunity to present and demonstrate its peaceful intentions but if it fails to take advantage of this opportunity it will face consequences."

"We hope all sides increase their diplomatic efforts, push the process of resolving the Iran nuclear issue diplomatically, and make progress," Chinese Foreign Ministry spokesman Qin Gang told reporters on Tuesday, adding China had noted the IAEA report.

November 17: Iran's building of a second uranium enrichment site is a "political message" that neither sanctions nor possible military attack will ever halt its nuclear program, a senior Iranian official said Tuesday.

Ali Asghar Soltanieh, Iran's envoy to the U.N. nuclear watchdog, told Reuters the agency's concern that Tehran may be hiding more nuclear work after it unveiled the enrichment site was an unfair political judgment beyond its mandate. He said Iran's disclosure of the site near Qom in September, being built in case its main Natanz enrichment plant was bombed, showed it was heeding transparency obligations to the International Atomic Energy Agency.

November17: Israel's Prime Minister Binyamin Netanyahu on Tuesday warned about the dangers of a nuclear Iran after touring a submarine believed capable of firing nuclear-tipped missiles. Netanyahu also visited a missile ship that led the seizure earlier this month of a ship which was loaded with Iranian weapons bound for Hizbullah.

Netanyahu told sailors aboard the ship INS Eilat "the threat that Iran poses is very grave for the state of Israel, for peace in the Middle East and the whole world." He said Israel would undoubtedly be the "first target, but not the last" in case of an Iranian attack.

November18: Iranian Foreign Minister Manouchehr Mottaki announced that Tehran would "definitely" not agree to send its low-enriched uranium abroad for further processing, AFP reported. According to the report, despite its rejection of the UN-brokered proposal, Iran may consider a fuel swap inside its borders.

November18: The United Nations nuclear watchdog has vehemently denied a report in the British newspaper The Times that it had been holding clandestine talks with Iran over its nuclear program. These talks, the report said, would "allow Tehran to retain the bulk of its nuclear program in return for co-operation with UN inspectors."

"These allegations are entirely baseless. It is regrettable that The Times should publish such a story without any effort to make a critical assessment of its source," the International Atomic Energy Agency said in a statement published on its website.

November19: U.S. President Barack Obama issued a strong warning to Iran on Thursday of consequences of its failure to respond to the offer of a nuclear deal and could have a package of steps to take "within weeks." "Iran has taken weeks now and has not shown its willingness to say yes to this proposal ... and so as a consequence we have begun discussions with our international partners about the importance of having consequences," Obama said at a joint news conference with South Korean President Lee Myung-bak during a visit to Seoul.

He said Iran would not be given an unlimited amount of time, likening the Iranian nuclear issue to the years of stop-and-start negotiations with North Korea about its nuclear ambitions. "We weren't going to duplicate what has happened with North Korea, in which talks just continue forever without any actual resolution to the issue," said Obama, who has advocated a policy of increased engagement, rather than confrontation, on thorny international issues.

Radiological Weapons

It is possible for a terrorist group to detonate a radiological or 'dirty bomb'. A 'dirty bomb' is composed of any radioactive source and a conventional explosive. The radioactive material is dispersed by the detonation of the explosive. Detonation of such a weapon is not as powerful as a nuclear blast, but can produce considerable radioactive fallout. There are other radiological weapons called radiological dispersal devices where an explosive is not necessary. A radiological weapon may be very appealing to terrorist groups as it is highly successful in instilling fear and panic amongst a population (particularly because of the threat of radiation poisoning), and would contaminate the immediate area for some period of time, disrupting attempts to repair the damage. The economic losses could be enormous - easily reaching into the tens of billions of dollars.

Chemical Weapons

Iran has experienced chemical warfare (CW) on the battlefield, suffering hundreds of thousands of casualties, both civilian and military, in chemical attacks during the Iran–Iraq War. As a result, Iran has promulgated a very public stance against the use of chemical weapons, making numerous vitriolic comments against Iraq's use of such weapons in international forums. Iran did not resort to using chemical weapons in retaliation for Iraqi chemical weapons attacks during the Iran–Iraq War, though it would have been legally entitled to do so under the then-existing international treaties on the use of chemical weapons which only prohibited the first use of such weapons. Following its experiences during the Iran–Iraq War, Iran signed the Chemical Weapons Convention on January 13, 1993 and ratified it on November 3, 1997. In the official declaration submitted to OPCW Iranian government admitted that it had produced mustard gas in 1980s but that ceased the offensive program and destroyed the stockpiles of operational weapons after the end of war with Iraq.

The Iran–Iraq War began in 1980 when Iraq attacked Iran. Early in the conflict, Iraq began to employ mustard gas and tabun delivered by bombs dropped from airplanes; approximately 5% of all Iranian casualties are directly attributable to the use of these agents.

About 100,000 Iranian soldiers were victims of Iraq's chemical attacks. Many were hit by mustard gas. The official estimate does not include the civilian population contaminated in bordering towns or the children and relatives of veterans, many of whom have developed blood, lung and skin complications, according to the Organization for Veterans. Nerve gas agents killed about 20,000 Iranian soldiers immediately, according to official reports. Of the 80,000 survivors, some 5,000 seek medical treatment regularly and about 1,000 are still hospitalized with severe, chronic conditions.

Despite the removal of Saddam and his regime by Coalition forces, there is deep resentment and anger in Iran that it was Western companies based in the Netherlands, West Germany, France, and the U.S. that helped Iraq develop its chemical weapons arsenal in the first place, and that the world did nothing to punish Iraq for its use of chemical weapons throughout the war.

Shortly before war ended in 1988, the Iraqi Kurdish village of Halabja was exposed to multiple chemical agents, killing about 5,000 of the town's 50,000 residents. After the incident, traces of mustard gas and the nerve agents sarin, tabun and VX were discovered.

During the Persian Gulf War in 1991, Coalition forces began a ground war in Iraq. Despite the fact that they did possess chemical weapons, Iraq did not use any chemical agents against coalition forces. The commander of the Allied Forces, Gen. H. Norman Schwarzkopf, suggested this may have been due to Iraqi fear of retaliation with nuclear weapons.

A U.S. Central Intelligence Agency report dated January 2001 speculated that Iran had manufactured and stockpiled chemical weapons - including blister, blood, choking, and probably nerve agents, and the bombs and artillery shells to deliver them. It further claimed that during the first half of 2001, Iran continued to seek production technology, training, expertise, equipment, and chemicals from entities in Russia and China that could be used to help Iran reach its goal of having indigenous nerve agent production capability. However the certainty of this assessment declined and in 2007 the U.S. Defense Intelligence Agency limited its public assessment to just noting that "Iran has a large and growing commercial chemical industry that could be used to support a chemical agent mobilization capability."

Missiles

Iran is believed to have a current inventory of 25 to 100 Shahab-3 missiles which have a range of 2100 km and are capable of being armed with conventional high explosive, submunition, chemical, biological, radiological dispersion and potentially nuclear warheads. A Shahab-4 with a range of 2000 km and a payload of 1000 kg is believed to be under development. Iran has stated the Shahab-3 is the last of its war missiles and the Shahab-4 is being developed to give the country the capability of launching communications and surveillance satellites. A Shahab-5, an intercontinental ballistic missile with a 10,000km range, is also believed to be under development.

Iran has 12 X-55 long range cruise missiles purchased without nuclear warheads from Ukraine in 2001. The X-55 has a range of 2500 to 3000 kilometers.

Iran's most advanced missile, the Fajr-3, has an unknown range but is estimated to be 2500 km. The missile is radar evading and can strike targets simultaneously using multiple warheads.

On November 2, 2006, Iran fired unarmed missiles to begin 10 days of military war games. Iranian state television reported "dozens of missiles were fired including Shahab-2 and Shahab-3 missiles. The missiles had ranges from 300 km to up to 2,000 km...Iranian experts have made some changes to Shahab-3 missiles installing cluster warheads in them with the capacity to carry 1,400 bombs." These launches come after some United States-led military exercises in the Persian Gulf on October 30,

2006, meant to train for blocking the transport of weapons of mass destruction.

On September 28, 2009, Iranian state television said the Revolutionary Guards, which controls Iran's missile program, successfully tested upgraded versions of the medium-range Shihab-3 and Sajjil-2 missiles. Both can carry nuclear warheads and can reach up to 2,000 kilometers, putting Israel, US military bases in the Middle East, and parts of Europe within striking distance.

The Sajjil-2 is Iran's most advanced two-stage surface-to-surface missile and is powered entirely by solid fuel, while the older Shihab-3 uses a combination of solid and liquid fuel in its most advanced form, which is also known as the Qadr-F1. The Sajjil's solid fuel propellant means it can be stored for significant amounts of time in underground missile silos prior to being launched. Experts say the Sajjil-2 is more accurate and has a more advanced navigation system than the Shahab.

Iran is in the midst of a multi-year plan that it hopes will culminate in the production of several hundred missile launchers and over 1,000 long-range ballistic missiles within the next six years, according to estimates in the Israeli defense establishment.

Green Salt Project

The Green Salt Project (also known as the "Project 1-11") is an alleged secretive Iranian entity focusing on uranium processing, high explosives and a missile warhead design. The Green Salt Project derives its name from uranium tetrafluoride, also known as green salt, an intermediate product in the conversion of uranium ore into uranium hexafluoride — a toxic gas that can undergo enrichment or purification into fuel for nuclear reactors or bombs. Since the International Atomic Energy Agency began investigating Iranian nuclear activities in 2002, the IAEA has discovered a series of clandestine nuclear activities, some of which violated Iran's safeguards agreement with the agency. The Green Salt Project is allegedly among these projects.

The Green Salt Project was initially brought to light by reports of a laptop computer in the CIA's possession which was supposedly smuggled out of Iran that contained a variety of information on Iran's alleged nuclear weapons program, from the design of underground testing facilities to schematics of nuclear missile warheads. The International Atomic Energy Agency (IAEA) referred to the green salt project on January 31, 2006, though the contents of the laptop have not been provided by the US to the IAEA for independent analysis or confirmation. IAEA officials reportedly remain suspicious of the information.

On 5 December 2005, the IAEA Secretariat had repeated its request for a meeting to discuss information that had been made available to the Secretariat about alleged nuclear research studies, including the Green Salt Project, as well as tests related to high explosives and the design of a missile re-entry vehicle, all of which could involve nuclear material and which appear to have administrative interconnections. On 16 December 2005, Iran replied that the "issues related to baseless allegations." Iran agreed on 23 January 2006 to a meeting with the Deputy Director-General for Safeguards for the clarification of the alleged Green Salt Project, but declined to address the other topics during that meeting. In the course of the meeting, which took place on 27 January 2006, the Agency presented for Iran's review a number of communications related to the project. Iran reiterated that all national nuclear projects are conducted by the Atomic Energy Organization of Iran (AEOI), that the allegations were baseless and that it would provide further clarifications later.

On 26 February 2006, the IAEA Deputy Director-General for Safeguards met with Iranian authorities to discuss the alleged Green Salt Project. Iran repeated that the allegations "are based on false and fabricated documents so they were baseless," and that neither such a project nor such studies exist or did exist.

The thing which nobody cares about is our planet.

The safe storage and disposal of nuclear waste is a significant challenge and yet unresolved problem. The most important waste stream from nuclear power plants is spent fuel. A large nuclear reactor produces 3 cubic metres (25–30 tonnes) of spent fuel each year. It is primarily composed of unconverted uranium as well as significant quantities of transuranic actinides (plutonium and curium, mostly). In addition, about 3% of it is made of fission products. The actinides (uranium, plutonium, and curium) are responsible for the bulk of the long term radioactivity, whereas the fission products are responsible for the bulk of the short term radioactivity.

Spent fuel is highly radioactive and needs to be handled with great care and forethought. However, spent nuclear fuel becomes less radioactive over the course of thousands of years of time. After about 5 percent of the rod has reacted the rod is no longer able to be used. Today, scientists are experimenting on how to recycle these rods to reduce waste. In the meantime, after 40 years, the radiation flux is 99.9% lower than it was the moment the spent fuel was removed, although still dangerously radioactive.

Spent fuel rods are stored in shielded basins of water (spent fuel pools), usually located on-site. The water provides both cooling for the still-decaying fission products, and shielding from the continuing radioactivity. After a few decades some on-site storage involves moving the now cooler, less radioactive fuel to a dry-storage facility or dry cask storage, where the fuel is stored in steel and concrete containers until its radioactivity decreases naturally ("decays") to levels safe enough for other processing. This interim stage spans years or decades or millennia, depending on the type of fuel. Most U.S. waste is currently stored in temporary storage sites requiring oversight, while suitable permanent disposal methods are discussed.

As of 2007, the United States had accumulated more than 50,000 metric tons of spent nuclear fuel from nuclear reactors. Underground storage at Yucca Mountain nuclear waste repository in U.S. has been proposed as permanent storage. After 10,000 years of radioactive decay, according to United States Environmental Protection Agency standards, the spent nuclear fuel will no longer pose a threat to public health and safety.

The amount of waste can be reduced in several ways, particularly reprocessing. Even so, the remaining waste will be substantially radioactive for at least 300 years even if the actinides are removed and for up to thousands of years if the actinides are left in. Even with separation of all actinides, and using fast breeder reactors to destroy by transmutation some of the longer-lived non-actinides as well, the waste must be segregated from the environment for one to a few hundred years, and therefore this is properly categorized as a long-term problem. Subcritical reactors or fusion reactors could also reduce the time the waste has to be stored. It has been argued that the best solution for the nuclear waste is above ground temporary storage since technology is rapidly changing. There is hope that current waste may well become a valuable resource in the future.

According to a 2007 story broadcast on 60 Minutes, nuclear power gives France the cleanest air of any industrialized country, and the cheapest electricity in all of Europe. France reprocesses its nuclear waste to reduce its mass and make more energy.

However, the article continues, "Today we stock containers of waste because currently scientists don't know how to reduce or eliminate the toxicity, but maybe in 100 years perhaps scientists will... Nuclear waste is an enormously difficult political problem which to date no country has solved. It is, in a sense, the Achilles heel of the nuclear industry... If France is unable to solve this issue, says Mandil, then 'I do not see how we can continue our nuclear program.'"Further, reprocessing itself has its critics, such as the Union of Concerned Scientists.

The nuclear industry also produces a huge volume of low-level radioactive waste in the form of contaminated items like clothing, hand tools, water purifier resins, and (upon decommissioning) the materials of which the reactor itself is built. In the United States, the Nuclear Regulatory Commission has repeatedly attempted to allow low-level materials to be handled as normal waste: landfilled, recycled into consumer items, et cetera. Most low-level waste releases very low levels of radioactivity and is only considered radioactive waste because of its history.

Reprocessing

Reprocessing can potentially recover up to 95% of the remaining uranium and plutonium in spent nuclear fuel, putting it into new mixed oxide fuel. This produces a reduction in long term radioactivity within the remaining waste, since this is largely short-lived fission products, and reduces its volume by over 90%. Reprocessing of civilian fuel from power reactors is currently done on large scale in Britain, France and (formerly) Russia, soon will be done in China and perhaps India, and is being done on an expanding scale in Japan. The full potential of reprocessing has not been achieved because it requires breeder reactors, which are not yet commercially available. France is generally cited as the most successful reprocessor, but it presently only recycles 28%

(by mass) of the yearly fuel use, 7% within France and another 21% in Russia.

Unlike other countries, the US stopped civilian reprocessing from 1976 to 1981 as one part of US non-proliferation policy, since reprocessed material such as plutonium could be used in nuclear weapons: however, reprocessing is now allowed in the U.S. Even so, in the U.S. spent nuclear fuel is currently all treated as waste.

In February, 2006, a new U.S. initiative, the Global Nuclear Energy Partnership was announced. It would be an international effort to reprocess fuel in a manner making nuclear proliferation unfeasible, while making nuclear power available to developing countries.

Depleted uranium

Uranium enrichment produces many tons of depleted uranium (DU) which consists of U-238 with most of the easily fissile U-235 isotope removed. U-238 is a tough metal with several commercial uses—for example, aircraft production, radiation shielding, and armor—as it has a higher density than lead. Depleted uranium is also useful in munitions as DU penetrators (bullets or APFSDS tips) "self sharpen", due to uranium's tendency to fracture along shear bands.

There are concerns that U-238 may lead to health problems in groups exposed to this material excessively, such as tank crews and civilians living in areas where large quantities of DU ammunition have been used in shielding, bombs, missile warheads, and bullets. In January 2003 the World Health Organization released a report finding that contamination from DU munitions were localized to a few tens of meters from the impact sites and contamination of local vegetation and water was 'extremely low'. The report also states that approximately 70% of ingested DU will leave the body after twenty four hours and 90% after a few days.

Proponents of nuclear energy

Proponents of nuclear energy contend that nuclear power is a sustainable energy source that reduces carbon emissions and increases energy security by decreasing dependence on foreign oil. Proponents also emphasize that the risks of storing waste are small and can be further reduced by using the latest technology in newer reactors and that the operational safety record of nuclear plants in the Western world is far better when compared to the other major types of power plants.

Critics believe that nuclear power is a potentially dangerous energy source, with decreasing proportion of nuclear energy in production, and dispute whether the risks can be reduced through new technology. Proponents advance the notion that nuclear power produces virtually no air pollution, in contrast to the chief viable alternative of fossil fuel combustion, and that nuclear waste storage technology virtually eliminates the risk of radiation leakage. Proponents also point out that nuclear power is the only viable course to achieve energy independence for most Western countries. Critics point to the issue of storing radioactive waste, the history of and continuing potential for radioactive contamination by accident or sabotage, the continuing possibility of nuclear proliferation, and the disadvantages of centralized electricity production. Arguments of economics and safety are used by both sides of the debate.

Nuclear proliferation

Nuclear proliferation is a term now used to describe the spread of nuclear weapons, fissile material, and weapons-applicable nuclear technology and information, to nations which are not recognized as "Nuclear Weapon States" by the Treaty on the Nonproliferation of Nuclear Weapons, also known as the Nuclear Nonproliferation Treaty or NPT.

Proliferation has been opposed by many nations with and without nuclear weapons, the governments of which fear that more countries with nuclear weapons may increase the possibility of nuclear warfare (up to and including the so-called "countervalue" targeting of civilians with nuclear weapons), destabilize international or regional relations, or infringe upon the national sovereignty of states.

Nuclear and radiation accidents

These accidents can hurt or kill almost anything that is around it while the accident is happening. In some cases, a release of radioactive contamination occurs, but in many cases the accident involves a sealed source or the release of radioactivity is small while the direct irradiation is large. Due to government and business secrecy, it is not always possible to determine with certainty the frequency or the extent of some events in the early days of the radiation industries. Modern misadventures, accidents, and incidents, which result in injury, death, or serious environmental contamination, tend to be well documented by the International Atomic Energy Agency.

Because of the different nature of the events it is best to divide the list into nuclear and radiation accidents. An example of nuclear accident might be one in which a reactor core is damaged such as in the Chernobyl Nuclear Power Plant Accident, while an example of a radiation accident might be some event such as a radiography accident where a worker drops the source into a river. These radiation accidents such as those involving the radiography sources often have as much or even greater ability to cause serious harm to both workers and the public than the well known nuclear accidents.

Radiation accidents are more common than nuclear accidents, and are often limited in scale. For instance at Soreq (Nuclear Research Center), a worker suffered a dose which was similar to one of the highest doses suffered by a worker on site at Chernobyl on day one. However, because the gamma source was never able to leave the 2-metre thick concrete enclosure, it was not able to harm many others.

The web page at the International Atomic Energy Agency, which deals with recent accidents are. The safety significance of nuclear accidents can be assessed and conveyed using the International Atomic Energy Agency International Nuclear Event Scale.

Serious Accidents

The worst nuclear accident in history is the Chernobyl Disaster that triggered the release of substantial amounts of radiation into the atmosphere in the form of both particle and gaseous radioisotopes, and is the most significant unintentional release of radiation into the environment to date. The Chernobyl disaster released as much as 400 times the radioactive contamination of the Atomic bombings of Hiroshima and Nagasaki. The explosion at the power station and subsequent fires inside the remains of the reactor provoked a radioactive cloud which drifted over Russia, Belarus and Ukraine, but also the European part of Turkey, Greece, Moldova, Romania, Bulgaria, Lithuania, Finland, Denmark, Norway, Sweden, Austria, Hungary, the Czech Republic and the Slovak Republic, Slovenia, Croatia, Poland, Switzerland, Germany, Italy, Ireland, France (including Corsica), Canada and the United Kingdom (UK). In fact, the initial evidence in other countries that a major exhaust of radioactive material had occurred came not from Soviet sources, but from Sweden, where on April 27 workers at the Forsmark Nuclear Power Plant (approximately 1100 km from the Chernobyl site) were found to have radioactive particles on their clothes. It was Sweden's search for the source of radioactivity, after they had determined there was no leak at the Swedish plant that led to the first hint of a serious nuclear problem in the Western Soviet Union. In France, the government then claimed that the radioactive cloud had stopped at the Italian border. Therefore, while some kinds of food (mushrooms in particular) were prohibited in Italy because of radioactivity, the French authorities took no such measures, in an attempt to appease the population's fears. Contamination from the Chernobyl disaster was not evenly spread across the surrounding countryside, but scattered irregularly depending on weather conditions. Reports from Soviet and Western scientists indicate that Belarus received about 60% of the contamination that fell on the former Soviet Union. A large area in Russia south of Bryansk was also contaminated, as were parts of northwestern Ukraine. 203 people were hospitalized immediately, of whom 31 died (28 of them died from acute radiation exposure). Most of these were fire and rescue workers trying to bring the disaster under control, who were not fully aware of how dangerous the radiation exposure (from the smoke) was (for a discussion of the more important isotopes in fallout see fission products). 135,000 people were evacuated from the area, including 50,000 from the nearby town of Pripyat, Ukraine. Health officials have predicted that over the next 70 years there will be a 2% increase in cancer rates in much of the population which was exposed to the 5-12 (depending on source) EBq of radioactive contamination released from the reactor. An additional 10 individuals have already died of cancer as a result of the disaster. A large swath of pine forest killed by acute radiation was named the Red Forest. The dead pines were bulldozed and buried. Livestock were removed during the human evacuations. Elsewhere in Europe, levels of radiation were examined in various natural foodstocks. In both Sweden and Finland, fish in deep freshwater lakes were banned for resale and landowners were advised not to consume certain types. Information regarding physical deformities in the plant and animal populations in the areas affected by radioactive fallout require capture and DNA testing of individuals to determine if abnormalities are the result of natural mutation, radiation poisoning, or exposure to other contaminants in the environment such as pesticides, industrial waste, or agricultural run-off.

An increased incidence of thyroid cancer among children in areas of Belarus, Ukraine and Russia affected by the Chernobyl disaster has been firmly established as a result of screening programs and, in the case of Belarus, an established cancer registry. The findings of most epidemiological studies must be considered interim, say experts, as analysis of the health effects of the disaster is an ongoing process. The activities undertaken by Belarus and Ukraine in response to the disaster — remediation of the environment, evacuation and resettlement, development of uncontaminated food sources and food distribution channels, and public health measures — have overburdened the governments of those countries. International agencies and foreign governments have provided extensive logistic and humanitarian assistance. In addition, the work of the European Commission and World Health Organization in strengthening the epidemiological research infrastructure in Russia, Ukraine and Belarus is laying the basis for major advances in these countries' ability to carry out epidemiological studies of all kinds. In September 2005, a comprehensive report was published by the Chernobyl Forum, comprising a number of agencies including the International Atomic Energy Agency (IAEA), the World Health Organization (WHO), United Nations bodies and the Governments of Belarus, the Russian Federation and Ukraine. This report titled: "Chernobyl's legacy: Health, Environmental and Socio-Economic Impacts", authored by about 100 recognized experts from many countries, put the total predicted number of deaths due to the disaster around 4,000 (of which 2,200 deaths are expected to be in the ranks of 200,000 liquidators). This predicted death toll includes the 47 workers who died of acute radiation syndrome as a direct result of radiation from the disaster, nine children who died from thyroid cancer and an estimated 4000 people who could die from cancer as a result of exposure to radiation. The report also stated that, apart from a 30 kilometers area around the site and a few restricted lakes and forests, radiation levels had returned to acceptable levels.

Other serious nuclear and radiation accident is the Mayak disaster, working conditions at Mayak resulted in severe health hazards and many accidents. The most notable accident occurred on 29 September 1957, when the failure of the cooling system for a tank storing tens of thousands of tons of dissolved nuclear waste resulted in a non-nuclear explosion having a force estimated at about 75 tons of TNT (310 gigajoules), which released some 2 Million Curies of radioactivity over 15,000 sq. miles. Subsequently, at least 200 people died of radiation sickness, 10,000 people were evacuated from their homes, and 470,000 people were exposed to radiation. People "grew hysterical with fear with the incidence of unknown 'mysterious' diseases breaking out. Victims were seen with skin 'sloughing off' their faces, hands and other exposed parts of their bodies." "Hundreds of square miles were left barren and unusable for decades and maybe centuries. Hundreds of people died, thousands were injured and surrounding areas were evacuated." This nuclear accident, the Soviet Union's worst before the Chernobyl disaster, is categorized as a level 6 "serious accident" on the 0-7 International Nuclear Events Scale.

Rumors of a nuclear mishap somewhere in the vicinity of Chelyabinsk had long been circulating in the West. That there had been a serious nuclear accident west of the Urals was eventually inferred from research on the effects of radioactivity on plants, animals, and ecosystems, published by Professor Leo Tumerman, former head of the Biophysics Laboratory at the Institute of Molecular Biology in Moscow, and associates. According to Gyorgy, who invoked the Freedom of Information Act to open up the relevant Central Intelligence Agency (CIA) files, the CIA knew of the 1957 Mayak accident all along, but kept it secret to prevent adverse consequences for the fledgling USA nuclear industry. "Ralph Nader surmised that the information had not been released because of the reluctance of the CIA to highlight a nuclear accident in the USSR that could cause concern among people living near nuclear facilities in the USA." Only in 1992, shortly after the fall of the USSR, did the Russians officially acknowledge the accident.

The Mayak Plant is associated with two other major nuclear accidents. The first occurred as a result of heavy rains causing Lake Karachay polluted with radioactive waste to release radioactive material into surrounding waters, and the second occurred in 1967 when wind spread dust from the bottom of Lake Karachay, a dried-up radioactively polluted lake (used as a dumping basin for Mayak's radioactive waste since 1951), over parts of Ozersk; over 400,000 people were irradiated.

Soviet Submarine K-431 Accident, Originally the Soviet submarine K-31, the K-431 was a Soviet nuclear-powered submarine that had a reactor accident on August 10, 1985. An explosion occurred during refueling of the submarine at Chazhma Bay, Vladivostok. TIME magazine has identified the accident as one of the world's "worst nuclear disasters".

Costa Rica Radiotherapy Accident, the radiotherapy accident in Costa Rica occurred with the Alycon II radiotherapy unit at San Juan de Dios Hospital in San Jose, Costa Rica. It was related to a Cobalt-60 source that was being used for radiotherapy in 1996.

In the course of the accident 114 patients received an overdose of radiation and 13 died of radiation-related injuries.

The Three Mile Island accident - The Three Mile Island accident of 1979 was a partial core meltdown in Unit 2 (a pressurized water reactor manufactured by Babcock & Wilcox) of the Three Mile Island Nuclear Generating Station in Dauphin County, Pennsylvania near Harrisburg. It was the most significant accident in the history of the American commercial nuclear power generating industry, resulting in the release of up to 481 PBq (13 million curies) of radioactive gases, but less than 740 GBq (20 curies) of the particularly dangerous iodine-131.

The accident began at 4:00 A.M. on Thursday, March 29, 1979, with failures in the non-nuclear secondary system, followed by a stuck-open pilot-operated relief valve (PORV) in the primary system, which allowed large amounts of reactor coolant to escape. The mechanical failures were compounded by the initial failure of plant operators to recognize the situation as a loss of coolant accident due to inadequate training and ambiguous control room indicators.

Three Mile Island Unit 2 was too badly damaged and contaminated to resume operations, the reactor was gradually deactivated and mothballed. TMI-2 had been online only three months but now had a ruined reactor vessel and a containment building that was unsafe to walk in and it has since been permanently closed. Cleanup started in August 1979 and officially ended in December 1993, having cost around US$975 million. Initially, efforts focused on the cleanup and decontamination of the site, especially the defueling of the damaged reactor. Starting in 1985 almost 100 tons of radioactive fuel were removed from the site, the defueling process was completed in 1990, and the damaged fuel was removed and disposed of in 1993.

Today, the TMI-2 reactor is permanently shut down and defueled, with the reactor coolant system drained, the radioactive water decontaminated and evaporated, radioactive waste shipped off-site to a disposal site, reactor fuel and core debris shipped off-site to a Department of Energy facility, and the remainder of the site being monitored. The owner says it will keep the facility in long-term, monitored storage until the operating license for the TMI-1 plant expires at which time both plants will be decommissioned. TMI-1's current license expires in 2014. On January 8, 2008, AmerGen Energy Corporation, the operator of TMI-1, submitted a license renewal application to the NRC. If the license is renewed, TMI-1's license will be extended to 2034.

Zaragoza Radiotherapy Accident - The radioactive accident at the Clinic of Zaragoza was a radiological accident that occurred between December 10 and 20, 1990 at the Clinic of Zaragoza, in Spain.

In the accident, at least 27 patients were injured and 11 of them died, according to International Atomic Energy Agency (IAEA). All of the injured were cancer patients receiving radiotherapy. On December 7, 1990 a technician performed maintenance on an electron accelerator at the Clinic of Zaragoza. On December 10, it returned to service after the repairs. On December 19, the Spanish Nuclear Safety Board was scheduled to make its annual review to the device, but due to bureaucratic reasons this review was delayed. The Spanish Nuclear Safety Board found the electron accelerator power was too high. The radiotherapy unit was repaired without following the correct instructions. The unit, in service 14 years at the time of the failure, had a breakdown in the electron beam accelerator control system ('deviator'). Repairs incorrectly increased output power, so patients that should have received therapy at 7 MeV instead were treated at 40 MeV. On December 20, 1990 the unit was stopped, restarting on March

8, 1991. Affected patients immediately suffered burns on the skin of the irradiated area, as well as inflammation of the internal organs and bone marrow. The first patient died on February 16, 1991, two months after irradiation. Fatalities increased until, on December 25, 1991, the last of a total of 25 patients died. However, the IAEA established that only eleven deaths were due to the faulty maintenance.

The number affected might have been higher, because 31 other cancer patients were receiving treatment with the proton accelerator, but the other unit at the clinic was in perfect working condition. The device continued working until December 1996, when it was switched off and scrapped. This was done discretely to avoid publicity.

Goiania Accident - The **Goiânia accident** was an incident of radioactive contamination in central Brazil that killed 4, injured 28, and produced over 200 cases of detectable radiation poisoning. On 13 September 1987, an old radiation source was scavenged from an abandoned hospital in Goiânia, the capital of the central Brazilian state of Goiás. It was subsequently handled by many people, resulting in four deaths and serious radioactive contamination of 249 other people. *Time* magazine has identified the accident as one of the world's "worst nuclear disasters".

Topsoil had to be removed from several sites, and several houses were demolished. All the objects from within those houses were removed and examined. Those that were found to be free of radioactivity were wrapped in plastic bags, while those that were contaminated were either decontaminated or disposed of as waste. In industry, the choice between decontaminating or disposing objects is based only on the economic value of the object and the ease of decontamination. The IAEA recognized in this case, however, that to reduce the psychological impact of the event, greater effort should be taken to clean up items of personal value, such as jewelry and photographs. It is not clear from the IAEA report to what degree this was practiced.

Church Rock Uranium Mill Spill - The Church Rock Uranium Mill Spill occurred in New Mexico, USA, in 1979.

On July 16, 1979 United Nuclear Corporation's Church Rock uranium mill tailings disposal pond breached its dam and 1100 tons of radioactive mill waste in approximately 93 million gallons of mine effluent flowed into the Rio Puerco. The contaminated water from the Church Rock spill travelled 80 miles downstream, reaching as far as Navajo, Arizona. Shortly after the breach below the dam radiation levels of river water were 7000 times that of the allowable level of drinking water. The flood backed up sewers, affected nearby aquifers and left stagnating pools on the riverside. Clean up was performed by state and federal criteria. However, according to Paul Robinson, research director at the Southwest Research and Information Center, only about 3,400 barrels of waste materials were retrieved (approximately 1%) and "very little of the spilled liquid was pumped out of the water supply". The spill resulted from "poor oversight, poor sitting and poor construction" and is an example of the problems that can occur at uranium mines and mills. The 50 ft. earthen dam was recognized as built on geologically unsound land by the corporation's consultant and Federal agencies. By 1977 cracks had appeared in the dam and went unreported to authorities. Although steps were taken at the time of the accident to notify the public in accordance with a state contingency plan local residents were not immediately aware of the toxic danger and were accustomed to using the riverside for recreation and herb gathering. Residents wading in the water went to the hospital complaining of burning feet and were diagnosed with heat stroke. Livestock were also found dying. Prior to the accident local residents used river water for irrigation and livestock. The eventual assistance of trucked in water ended in 1981 and farmers were then left with little choice other than to resume use of the river. For some types of cancers Navaho have a significantly higher rate than the national average. Yet, no epidemiological studies have been done at Church Rock. In terms of the amount of radiation released the accident was comparable in magnitude to the Three Mile Island accident of the same year and has been reported as "the largest radioactive accident in U.S. History". A peer reviewed article in the American Journal of Public Health in 2007 proposed that the stark lack of peer-reviewed studies of health effects of the accident when compared to well studied events such as Three Mile Island may be related to both the "early stage in the nuclear cycle" (mining, milling and processing) dependent on a large numbered labor-force and "low-income rural American Indian communities".

The Northeast Church Rock Mine site is now part of the Environmental Protection Agency's Superfund investigation and cleanup effort.

Other serious nuclear and radiation accidents include Soviet submarine K-19 accident, Windscale fire and the SL-1 accident.

Accident Types

Criticality Accidents

A criticality accident (also sometimes referred to as an "excursion" or "power excursion") occurs when a nuclear chain reaction is accidentally allowed to occur in fissile material, such as enriched uranium or plutonium. The Chernobyl accident is an example of a criticality accident. This accident destroyed a reactor at the plant and left a large geographic area uninhabitable. In a smaller scale accident at Sarov a technician working with highly enriched uranium was irradiated while preparing an experiment involving a sphere of fissile material. The Sarov accident is interesting because the system remained critical for many days before it could be stopped, though safely located in a shielded experimental hall. This is an example of a limited scope accident where only a few people can be harmed, while no release of radioactivity into the environment occurred. A criticality accident with limited off site release of both radiation (gamma and neutron) and a very small release of radioactivity occurred at Tokaimura in 1999 during the production of enriched uranium fuel. Two workers died, a third was permanently injured, and 350 citizens were exposed to radiation.

Decay Heat

Decay heat accidents are where the heat generated by the radioactive decay causes harm. In a large nuclear reactor, a loss of coolant accident can damage the core: for example, at Three Mile Island a recently shutdown PWR (Pressurized water reactor) reactor was left for a length of time without cooling water. As a result the nuclear fuel was damaged, and the core partly melted. The removal of the decay heat is a significant reactor safety concern, especially shortly after shutdown. Failure to remove decay heat may cause the reactor core temperature to rise to dangerous levels and has caused nuclear accidents. The heat removal is usually achieved through several redundant and diverse systems, and the heat is often dissipated to an 'ultimate heat sink' which has a large capacity and requires no active power, though this method is typically used after decay heat has reduced to a very small value. However, the main cause of release of radioactivity in the Three Mile Island accident was a Pilot-Operated Relief Valve on the primary loop which stuck in the open position. This caused the overflow tank into which it drained to rupture and release large amounts of radioactive cooling water into the Containment Building.

Fartash Barvarz

Transport

Transport accidents can cause a release of radioactivity resulting in contamination or shielding to be damaged resulting in direct irradiation. In Cochabamba a defective gamma radiography set was transported in a passenger bus as cargo. The gamma source was outside the shielding, and it irradiated some bus passengers.

In the United Kingdom, it was revealed in a court case that in March 2002 a radiotherapy source was transported from Leeds to Sellafield with defective shielding. The shielding had a gap on the underside. It is thought that no human has been seriously harmed by the escaping radiation.

Equipment Failure

Equipment failure is one possible type of accident, recently at Białystok in Poland the electronics associated with a particle accelerator used for the treatment of cancer suffered a malfunction. This then led to the overexposure of at least one patient. While the initial failure was the simple failure of a semiconductor diode, it set in motion a series of events which led to a radiation injury.

Human Error

Human error has been responsible for some accidents, such as when a person miscalculated the activity of a teletherapy source. This then led to patients being given the wrong dose of gamma rays. In the case of radiotherapy accidents, an underexposure is as much an accident as an overexposure as the patients may not get the full benefit of the prescribed treatment. Also, humans have made errors while attempting to service plants and equipment which has resulted in overdoses of radiation, such as the Nevvizh and Soreq irradiator accidents.

In 1946 Canadian Manhattan Project physicist Louis Slotin performed a risky experiment known as "tickling the dragon's tail" which involved two hemispheres of neutron-reflective beryllium being brought together around a plutonium core to bring it to criticality. Against operating procedures, the hemispheres were separated only by a screwdriver. The screwdriver slipped and set off a chain reaction criticality accident filling the room with harmful radiation and a flash of blue light (caused by excited, ionized air particles returning to their unexcited states). Slotin reflexively separated the hemispheres in reaction to the heat flash and blue light, preventing further irradiation of several co-workers present in the room. However Slotin absorbed a lethal dose of the radiation and died nine days afterwards.

Lost Source

Lost source accidents are ones in which a radioactive source is lost, stolen or abandoned. The source then might cause harm to humans or the environment. For example, see the event in Lilo where sources were left behind by the Soviet army. Another case occurred at Yanango where a radiography source was lost, also at Samut Prakarn a cobalt-60 teletherapy source was lost and at Gilan in Iran a radiography source harmed a welder. The best known example of this type of event is the Goiânia accident which occurred in Brazil.

The International Atomic Energy Agency has provided guides for scrap metal collectors on what a sealed source might look like. The scrap metal industry is the one where lost sources are most likely to be found.

Fartash Barvarz

Uranium Mining

Uranium mining is the process of extraction of uranium ore from the ground. As uranium ore is mostly present at relatively low concentrations, most uranium mining is very volume-intensive, and thus tends to be undertaken as open-pit mining. It is also undertaken in only a small number of countries of the world, as the resource is rare.

There are many uranium mines operating around the world, in some twenty countries, though more than two thirds of world production comes from just ten mines. Most of the uranium ore deposits at present supporting these mines have average grades in excess of 0.10% of uranium - that is, greater than 1000 parts per million. In the first phase of uranium mining to the 1960s, this would have been seen as a respectable grade, but today some Canadian mines have huge amounts of ore up to 20% U average grade. Other mines however can operate successfully with very low grade ores. Generally speaking, uranium mining is no different from other kinds of mining unless the ore is very high grade.

Intensive exploration for uranium started after the end of World War II as a result of the military and civilian demand for uranium. There were three separate periods of uranium exploration or "booms." These were from 1956 to 1960, 1967 to 1971, and from 1976 to 1982.

In the 20th century the United States was the world's largest uranium producer. Grants Uranium District in northwestern New Mexico was the largest United States uranium producer. The Gas Hills Uranium District was the second largest uranium producer. The famous Lucky Mc Mine is located in the Gas Hills near Riverton, Wyoming. Canada has since surpassed the United States as the cumulative largest producer in the world.

In India, Nalgonda District, the Rajiv Gandhi Tiger Reserve (the only tiger project in Andhra Pradesh) has been forced to surrender over 1,000 sq. kilometers to uranium mining following a directive from the Central Ministry of Environment and Forests. In 2007, India was able to extract 229 tonnes of U3O8 from its soil.

In Northern regions, The Meghalaya government has decided to lease out 422 hectares of land in the West Khasi Hills region for 30 years to the Uranium Corporation of India Limited (UCIL) for pre-project developmental works, a step which is agitating a number of locals.

According to locals, Meghalaya's environment has been destroyed by the through unscientific mining of coal, limestone and other natural resources.

They claim that uranium mining will only add to environmental degradation of Meghalaya.

Buddha Weeps in Jadugoda (1999)

Shriprakash was born on the 23rd of December 1966 from a family of farmers in the state of Bihar, in an area that in 2000 became a separate state called Jharkhand. He graduated in Science and Journalism from Ranchi University and soon became interested in video as an activist medium. With his films he has attempted to capture the struggles and aspirations of indigenous local communities in Bihar and Jharkhand, and to give them a voice. "I do not impose my views," he explains. "I am only the instrument that takes the camera to the place of struggle. It's the people participating in the struggle who actually make the film. They live out their lives and voice their concerns in their own words. I only record."

Jadugoda is an area in the state of Bihar populated by Adivasi (tribal peoples of India). It first came into prominence when uranium deposits were discovered in the area, since Jadugoda is India's only underground uranium mine. The film documents the devastating effects of uranium mining by Uranium Corporation of India Limited in Jadugoda. For the last thirty years, the radioactive wastes have been just dumped into the rice fields of the Adivasis. The government agency mining the uranium makes no attempt to protect the lives of the people and environment of the area. The unsafe mining of uranium has resulted in excessive radiation which has led to genetic mutations and slow deaths. Medical reports reveal that the impact of radiation on the health of tribal peoples has already been devastating. The film is an attempt to record the tragedy that has played havoc with the lives of the people of Jadugoda.

Shriprakash doesn't use grants or loans for his films, instead he relies on food and transport provided by the local communities themselves, who use his finished film to strengthen the resolve of their own people and lobby their cause in different form. Post-production funds are raised from well-wishers and by selling CD copies of the films to NGOs and activist groups who use the films as motivational and training tools. As for the initial investment on a video camera, it was raised through a business that he started in Ranchi with some like-minded friends in the 1980s: video-shooting marriages and other functions, to pay for the kind of films they wanted to make. Since the business didn't work, the group dissolved and Shriprakash moved to Delhi, where he works on making video films for NGOs.

On Aug. 10, 2008, Atomic Energy Commission chairman Anil Kakodkar laid foundation stone for the mine at Tummaplapalli village in Kadapa. The Uranium Corp of India Ltd (UCIL) is building the mine and mill at a cost of Rs 11.29 billion ($268.8 million). It would have a capacity to produce 150,000 tonnes of uranium a year. The project would be completed "as early as possible", Kakodkar told reporters on the occasion. He tried to allay apprehensions in some quarters that the mine would be harmful to environment and public health. "We will take care of (people's) safety. There need be no apprehensions. It will have no impact on environment or people," said Kakodkar, who is also the secretary of the Department of Atomic Energy. Several environmental groups have raised apprehensions that the mine would impact the environment and the health of people living in nearby villages. They alleged that several of their activists were beaten up by the police during the mandatory public hearing held in 2006, to silence their protest. (The Economic Times Aug. 10, 2008)

In a press release, members of the NGO mines, minerals & People (mm&P) said "a public hearing based on irrelevant pronouncements is a mere formality and cannot be construed as obtaining the consent of people in a democratic manner." Nearly a million tonnes of waste would have to be disposed off every year and "the design of the tailing pond is incremental, which can be disastrous." They also questioned the need for taking up such mining in a densely populated area in the Kadapa district. "The Tummaplapalli Uranium Project will be in one of the densely inhabited regions, compared to the existing and proposed uranium mines in India and a deeper (and proper) inquiry into the environmental impact is called for". According to them, over 12000 people in the region would be affected and they should not be exposed to radiation and other risks. They appealed to the Government to get the EIA done again, taking into account these aspects. (The Hindu Business Line 11 Sep 2006)

Gogi Mine (Gulbarga district-Karnataka) - Shahapur taluk (county) tax collector Janardhan Upadhya confirmed that they had received a letter from Atomic Research Centre (ARC), Hyderabad, asking for requisition of 100 acres of land. He said the revenue department would submit a proposal to the Karnataka government so that they could acquire the land, using the "Urgency Clause", under section 17 of the Land Acquisition Act since the Union government needed the land. But the Gogi gram panchayat (local government) is up in arms over the proposal to mine uranium in the village. It has decided to request the government to instruct ARC to close its survey/ mining work in the village. The local government in its resolution has said that many people were suffering from skin diseases as effluents from drilling were mixing with the drinking water; they said that drilling was polluting water in the bore-wells as well. (ExpressBuzz June 30, 2009)

Future of the Industry

According to the World Nuclear Association, globally during the 1980s one new nuclear reactor started up every 17 days on average, and by the year 2015 this rate could increase to one every 5 days. Many countries remain active in developing nuclear power, including Pakistan, Japan, China and India, all actively developing both fast and thermal technology, South Korea and the United States, developing thermal technology only, and South Africa and China, developing versions of the Pebble Bed Modular Reactor (PBMR). Several EU member states actively pursue nuclear programs, while some other member states continue to have a ban for the nuclear energy use. Japan has an active nuclear construction program with new units brought on-line in 2005.

There is a possible impediment to production of nuclear power plants as only a few companies worldwide have the capacity to forge single-piece containment vessels, which reduce the risk of a radiation leak. Utilities across the world are submitting orders years in advance of any actual need for these vessels. Other manufacturers are examining various options, including making the component themselves, or finding ways to make a similar item using alternate methods. Other solutions include using designs that do not require single-piece forged pressure vessels such as Canada's Advanced CANDU Reactors or Sodium-cooled Fast Reactors.

The World Nuclear Industry Status Report 2009 states that "even if Finland and France each builds a reactor or two, China goes for an additional 20 plants and Japan, Korea or Eastern Europe add a few units, the overall worldwide trend will most likely be downwards over the next two decades". With long lead times of 10 years or more, it will be difficult to maintain or increase the number of operating nuclear power plants over the next 20 years. The one exception to this outcome would be if operating lifetimes could be substantially increased beyond 40 years on average. This seems unlikely since the present average age of the operating nuclear power plant fleet in the world is 25 years.

However, China plans to build more than 100 plants, while in the US the licenses of almost half its reactors have already been extended to 60 years, and plans to build more than 30 new ones are under consideration. Further, the U.S. NRC and the U.S. Department of Energy have initiated research into Light water reactor sustainability which is hoped will lead to allowing extensions of reactor licenses beyond 60 years, in increments of 20 years, provided that safety can be maintained, as the loss in non-CO_2-emitting generation capacity by retiring reactors "may serve to challenge U.S. energy security, potentially resulting in increased greenhouse gas emissions, and contributing to an imbalance between electric supply and demand." In 2008, the International Atomic Energy Agency (IAEA) predicted that nuclear power capacity could double by 2030, though that would not be enough to increase nuclear's share of electricity generation.

Fartash Barvarz

Nuclear Energy versus Other renewable forms

Renewable energy is energy generated from natural resources such as sunlight, wind, rain, tides, and geothermal heat, which are renewable (naturally replenished). In 2006, about 18% of global final energy consumption came from renewable, with 13% coming from traditional biomass, such as wood-burning. Hydroelectricity was the next largest renewable source, providing 3% of global energy consumption and 15% of global electricity generation.

Wind power is growing at the rate of 30 percent annually, with a worldwide installed capacity of 121,000 megawatts (MW) in 2008, and is widely used in European countries and the United States. The annual manufacturing output of the photovoltaics industry reached 6,900 MW in 2008, and photovoltaic (PV) power stations are popular in Germany and Spain. Solar thermal power stations operate in the USA and Spain, and the largest of these is the 354 MW SEGS power plant in the Mojave Desert. The world's largest geothermal power installation is The Geysers in California, with a rated capacity of 750 MW. Brazil has one of the largest renewable energy programs in the world, involving production of ethanol fuel from sugar cane, and ethanol now provides 18 percent of the country's automotive fuel. Ethanol fuel is also widely available in the USA.

While most renewable energy projects and production is large-scale, renewable technologies are also suited to small off-grid applications, sometimes in rural and remote areas, where energy is often crucial in human development. Kenya has the world's highest household solar ownership rate with roughly 30,000 small (20–100 watt) solar power systems sold per year.

Wind Power

Airflows can be used to run wind turbines. Modern wind turbines range from around 600 kW to 5 MW of rated power, although turbines with rated output of 1.5–3 MW have become the most common for commercial use; the power output of a turbine is a function of the cube of the wind speed, so as wind speed increases, power output increases dramatically. Areas where winds are stronger and more constant, such as offshore and high altitude sites, are preferred locations for wind farms. Typical capacity factors are 20-40%, with values at the upper end of the range in particularly favorable sites.

Globally, the long-term technical potential of wind energy is believed to be five times total current global energy production, or 40 times current electricity demand. This could require large amounts of land to be used for wind turbines, particularly in areas of higher wind resources. Offshore resources experience mean wind speeds of 90% greater than that of land, so offshore resources could contribute substantially more energy. This number could also increase with higher altitude ground-based or airborne wind turbines.

Wind power is renewable and produces no greenhouse gases during operation, such as carbon dioxide and methane.

Water Power

Energy in water (in the form of kinetic energy, temperature differences or salinity gradients) can be harnessed and used. Since water is about 800 times denser than air, even a slow flowing stream of water, or moderate sea swell, can yield considerable amounts of energy.

Fartash Barvarz

Solar Energy

World's largest photovoltaic power plants

As of January 2009, the largest photovoltaic (PV) power plants in the world are the Parque Fotovoltaico Olmedilla de Alarcon (Spain, 60 MW), the Moura photovoltaic power station (Portugal, 46 MW), and the Waldpolenz Solar Park (Germany, 40 MW). Several other PV power plants were completed in Spain in 2008: Planta Solar Arnedo (30 MW), Parque Solar Merida/Don Alvaro (30 MW), Planta solar Fuente Álamo (26 MW), Planta fotovoltaica de Lucainena de las Torres (23.2 MW), Parque Fotovoltaico Abertura Solar (23.1 MW), Parque Solar Hoya de Los Vincentes (23 MW), Huerta Solar Almaraz (22.1 MW), Solarpark Calveron (21 MW), and the Planta Solar La Magascona (20 MW).

Topaz Solar Farm is a proposed 550 MW solar photovoltaic power plant which is to be built northwest of California Valley in the USA at a cost of over $1 billion. Built on 9.5 square miles (25 km2) of ranchland, the project would utilize thin-film PV panels designed and manufactured by OptiSolar in Hayward and Sacramento. The project would deliver approximately 1,100 gigawatt-hours (GW·h) annually of renewable energy. The project is expected to begin construction in 2010, begin power delivery in 2011, and be fully operational by 2013. High Plains Ranch is a proposed 250 MW solar photovoltaic power plant which is to be built by SunPower in the Carrizo Plain, northwest of California Valley.

However, when it comes to renewable energy systems and PV, it is not just large systems that matter. Building-integrated photovoltaics or "onsite" PV systems have the advantage of being matched to end use energy needs in terms of scale. So the energy is supplied close to where it is needed.

Biofuel

Plants use photosynthesis to grow and produce biomass. Also known as biomatter, biomass can be used directly as fuel or to produce biofuels. Agriculturally produced biomass fuels, such as biodiesel, ethanol and bagasse (often a by-product of sugar cane cultivation) can be burned in internal combustion engines or boilers. Typically biofuel is burned to release its stored chemical energy. Research into more efficient methods of converting biofuels and other fuels into electricity utilizing fuel cells is an area of very active work.

Liquid biofuel is usually either a bioalcohol such as ethanol fuel or an oil such as biodiesel or straight vegetable oil. Biodiesel can be used in modern diesel vehicles with little or no modification to the engine. It can be made from waste and virgin vegetable and animal oils and fats (lipids). Virgin vegetable oils can be used in modified diesel engines. In fact the diesel engine was originally designed to run on vegetable oil rather than fossil fuel. A major benefit of biodiesel use is the reduction in net CO_2 emissions, since all the carbon emitted was recently captured during the growing phase of the biomass. The use of biodiesel also reduces emission of carbon monoxide and other pollutants by 20 to 40%.

In some areas corn, cornstalks, sugarbeets, sugar cane, and switchgrasses are grown specifically to produce ethanol (also known as grain alcohol) a liquid which can be used in internal combustion engines and fuel cells. Ethanol is being phased into the current energy infrastructure. E85 is a fuel composed of 85% ethanol and 15% gasoline that is sold to consumers. Biobutanol is being developed as an alternative to bioethanol.

Geothermal Energy

The geothermal energy from the core of the Earth is closer to the surface in some areas than in others. Where hot underground steam or water can be tapped and brought to the surface it may be used to generate electricity. Such geothermal power sources exist in certain geologically unstable parts of the world such as Chile, Iceland, New Zealand, United States, the Philippines and Italy. The two most prominent areas for this in the United States are in the Yellowstone basin and in northern California. Iceland produced 170 MW geothermal power and heated 86% of all houses in the year 2000 through geothermal energy. Some 8000 MW of capacity is operational in total.

Transport Issues and Release of radioactivity from fuel

The IAEA assume that under normal operation the coolant of water cooled reactor will contain some radioactivity but during a reactor accident the coolant radioactivity level may rise. The IAEA state that under a series of different conditions different amounts of the core inventory can be released from the fuel, the four conditions the IAEA consider are normal operation, a spike in coolant activity due to a sudden shutdown/loss of pressure (core remains covered with water), a cladding failure resulting in the release of the activity in the fuel/cladding gap (this could be due to the fuel being uncovered by the loss of water for 15–30 minutes where the cladding reached a temperature of 650-1250 C) or a melting of the core (the fuel will have to be uncovered for at least 30 minutes, and the cladding would reach a temperature in excess of 1650 C).

Based upon the assumption that a PWR contains 300 tons of water, and that the activity of the fuel of a 1 GWe reactor is as the IAEA predict, then the coolant activity after an accident such as the three mile island accident where a core is uncovered and then recovered with water then the resulting activity of the coolant can be predicted.

High-level radioactive waste

Spent fuel is highly radioactive and needs to be handled with great care and forethought. However, spent nuclear fuel becomes less radioactive over the course of thousands of years of time. After about 5 percent of the rod has reacted the rod is no longer able to be used. Today, scientists are experimenting on how to recycle these rods to reduce waste. In the meantime, after 40 years, the radiation flux is 99.9% lower than it was the moment the spent fuel was removed, although still dangerously radioactive.

Spent fuel rods are stored in shielded basins of water (spent fuel pools), usually located on-site. The water provides both cooling for the still-decaying fission products, and shielding from the continuing radioactivity. After a few decades some on-site storage involves moving the now cooler, less radioactive fuel to a dry-storage facility or dry cask storage, where the fuel is stored in steel and concrete containers until its radioactivity decreases naturally ("decays") to levels safe enough for other processing. This interim stage spans years or decades or millennia, depending on the type of fuel. Most U.S. waste is currently stored in temporary storage sites requiring oversight, while suitable permanent disposal methods are discussed.

As of 2007, the United States had accumulated more than 50,000 metric tons of spent nuclear fuel from nuclear reactors. Underground storage at Yucca Mountain nuclear waste repository in U.S. has been proposed as permanent storage. After 10,000 years of radioactive decay, according to United States

Environmental Protection Agency standards, the spent nuclear fuel will no longer pose a threat to public health and safety.

Alleged Nuclear Terrorism attempts and Plans

In June 2002, U.S. citizen Jose Padilla was arrested for allegedly planning a radiological attack on the city of Chicago; however, he was never charged with such conduct. He was instead convicted of charges that he conspired to "murder, kidnap and maim" people overseas.

In November 2006, MI5 warned that Islamic terrorists, specifically the al-Qaida were planning on using nuclear weapons against cities in the United Kingdom by obtaining the bombs via clandestine means.

In June 2007, the FBI released to the press the name of Adnan Gulshair el Shukrijumah, allegedly the operations leader for developing tactical plans for detonating nuclear bombs in several American cities simultaneously.

The murder of Litvinenko with radioactive polonium "represents an ominous landmark: the beginning of an era of nuclear terrorism," according to Andrew J. Patterson.

Security specialist Shaun Gregory argued in an article that terrorists have attacked Pakistani nuclear facilities three times in the recent past; twice in 2007 and once in 2008.

In August 2002, the United States launched a program to track and secure enriched uranium from 24 Soviet-style reactors in 16 countries, in order to reduce the risk of the materials falling into the hands of terrorists or "rogue states". The first such operation was Project Vinca, "a multinational, public-private effort to remove nuclear material from a poorly secured Yugoslav research institute." The project has been hailed as "a nonproliferation success story" with the "potential to inform broader 'global cleanout' efforts to address one of the weakest links in the nuclear nonproliferation chain: insufficiently secured civilian nuclear research facilities."

In the German case, a man attempted to poison his ex-wife with plutonium stolen from WAK (Wiederaufbereitungsanlage Karlsruhe), a small scale reprocessing plant where he worked. He did not steal a large amount of plutonium, just some rags used for wiping surfaces and a small amount of liquid waste. The man was eventually sent to prison. At least two people (besides the criminal) were contaminated by the plutonium. Two flats in Landau in the Rhineland-Palatinate were contaminated, and had to be cleaned at a cost of two million euro. Photographs of the case and details of other nuclear crimes have been presented by a worker at the Institute for Transuranium Elements.

Criminal use of X-ray equipment and other radiation technology by Secret Police

Some former East German dissidents claim that the Stasi used X-ray equipment to induce cancer in political prisoners.

Similarly, some anti-Castro activists claim that the Cuban secret police sometimes used radioactive isotopes to induce cancer in "adversaries they wished to destroy with as little notice as possible". In 1997, the Cuban expatriate columnist Carlos Alberto Montaner called this method "the Bulgarian Treatment", after its alleged use by the Bulgarian secret police.

Fartash Barvarz

Trafficking in radioactive and nuclear materials

Information reported to the International Atomic Energy Agency (IAEA) shows "a persistent problem with the illicit trafficking in nuclear and other radioactive materials, thefts, losses and other unauthorized activities".

From 1993 to 2006, the IAEA confirmed 1080 illicit trafficking incidents reported by participating countries. Of the 1080 confirmed incidents, 275 incidents involved unauthorized possession and related criminal activity, 332 incidents involved theft or loss of nuclear or other radioactive materials, 398 incidents involved other unauthorized activities, and in 75 incidents the reported information was not sufficient to determine the category of incident. Several hundred additional incidents have been reported in various open sources, but are not yet confirmed.

Quack Medicine

In the early 20th century a series of "medical" products which contained radioactive elements were marketed to the general public. These are included in this discussion of nuclear/radioactive crime because the sale and production of these products is now covered by criminal law. Because some perfectly good radioactive medical products exist, (such as iodine-131 for the treatment of cancer), it is important to note that sale of products similar to those described below is criminal, as they are unlicensed medicines.

Radithor, well known patent medicine/snake oil, is possibly the best known example of radioactive quackery. It consisted of triple distilled water containing at a minimum 1 microcurie each of the radium 226 and 228 isotopes.

Radithor was manufactured from 1918 - 1928 by the Bailey Radium Laboratories, Inc., of East Orange, New Jersey. The head of the laboratories was listed as Dr. William J. A. Bailey, not a medical doctor. It was advertised as "A Cure for the Living Dead" as well as "Perpetual Sunshine".

Radioactive scrap metal

Radioactive scrap metal is the situation when radioactive material enters the metal recycling process known as the "scrap metal trade". A lost source accident is one where a radioactive object is lost or stolen. Such objects often end up in the scrap metal industry, as people mistake them for harmless bits of metal. The International Atomic Energy Agency has provided guides for scrap metal collectors on what a sealed source might look like. The best known example of this type of event is the Goiânia accident, in Brazil.

While some lost source accidents have not involved the scrap metal industry, they are still good examples of the likely scale and scope of a lost source accident. For example, the Red Army left sources behind in Lilo. Another case occurred at Yanango where a radiography source was lost and at Gilan, Iran a radiography source harmed a welder.

An alternative danger to the accidental loss of small amounts of highly radioactive metal is deliberate use of large amounts of low level radioactive sources. The US army has used thousands of tonnes of DU (Depleted uranium) munitions, often in cities, especially in Iraq.

Radioactive sources have a wide range of uses in medicine and industry, it is common for the design (and nature) of a source to be tailored to the application so it is impossible to state with confidence what the "typical" source looks like or contains.

Tammiku (Estonia)

In Tammiku (Estonia) a group of three men were responsible for a similar incident: they burgled a radioactive waste store to steal scrap metal. One of them picked up a metal pipe and placed it in his pocket. This metal pipe was a very strong 137Cs source which gave a high localised dose to the man's leg (1800 Sv local, 4 Sv whole body). He was admitted a few days later to hospital where he claimed to have had an accident in the woods. He died shortly after as a result of whole body irradiation from the source. Before going to the hospital, he left the source in his house where it then irradiated other members of his family and his dog (which died as a result). His son suffered a localised radiation burn (local dose of 25 Sv, whole body 3.6 Gy) which resulted in the amputation of fingers, when he inadvertently handled the source when looking for tools to repair his bicycle. When a medical doctor saw these burns it was understood that an ionising radiation accident was in progress. The man's wife got a 500 mSv dose while his mother got a 2.25 Sv dose.

It is interesting to note that the scrap metal industry was involved twice in this: the caesium source being originally found in a shipment of scrap metal which was brought into the country (at that point it was thought to be a 60Co source based on half thickness measurements). The source was placed in the radioactive waste store for safekeeping, which was subsequently entered by the men who were intent on stealing scrap metal.

In the Tammiku event, where a caesium source of similar strength was stolen, the accident site was easy to clean because the source remained sealed. All that needed to be done was to pick the source up, place it in a lead pot and transport this to the radioactive waste store. It is noteworthy that in that case the source recovery workers wore rubber gloves, but more importantly failed to use tongs. Gamma rays obey the inverse square law so by slightly increasing the distance between the recovery worker and the source the dose rate experienced by the worker can be reduced. In the recovery of lost sources the International Atomic Energy Agency consider that it is best to plan the recovery first, and to consider using a crane or other device to place shielding (such as pallet of bricks or a concrete block) near the source to allow the recovery worker to walk up to it while being protected by the added shielding.

Russian suitcase nukes

In 1997, former Russian National Security Advisor Alexander Lebed made public claims about lost "suitcase nukes" following the dissolution of the Soviet Union. In an interview with the newsmagazine 60 Minutes, Lebed said: I'm saying that more than a hundred weapons out of the supposed number of 250 are not under the control of the armed forces of Russia. I don't know their location. I don't know whether they have been destroyed or whether they are stored or whether they've been sold or stolen, I don't know.

However, the Russian government immediately rejected Lebed's claims. Russia's atomic energy ministry went so far as to dispute that suitcase nuclear weapons had even ever been developed by the Soviet Union. Later testimony however insinuated that the suitcase bombs had been under the control of the KGB and not the army or the atomic energy ministry, so they might not know of their existence. Russian president Vladimir Putin, in an interview with Barbara Walters in 2001, stated about suitcase nukes, "I don't really believe this is true. These are just legends.

One can probably assume that somebody tried to sell some nuclear secrets. But there is no documentary confirmation of those developments."

The highest-ranking GRU defector Stanislav Lunev claimed that such Russian-made devices do exist and described them in more detail. These devices, "identified as RA-115s (or RA-115-01s for submersible weapons)" weigh from fifty to sixty pounds. They can last for many years if wired to an electric source. In case there is a loss of power, there is a battery backup. If the battery runs low, the weapon has a transmitter that sends a coded message—either by satellite or directly to a GRU post at a Russian embassy or consulate." According to Lunev, the number of "missing" nuclear devices (as found by General Lebed) "is almost identical to the number of strategic targets upon which those bombs would be used."

Heat Generation

The reactor core generates heat in a number of ways:

The kinetic energy of fission products is converted to thermal energy when these nuclei collide with nearby atoms.

Some of the gamma rays produced during fission are absorbed by the reactor, their energy being converted to heat.

Heat produced by the radioactive decay of fission products and materials that have been activated by neutron absorption. This decay heat source will remain for some time even after the reactor is shutdown.

The heat power generated by the nuclear reaction is 1,000,000 times that of the equal mass of coal.

Now I'll let you, my readers to sum up and get a result out of the book. What I believe, Nuclear Power in any form is like a decayed tooth which you try to go on with because you really don't want to go to dentist. At the end you have to go because the pain is started. If today Human decide to stop what they did in the nuclear industry the influences of the radioactive wastes, they'll be with us until another 10,000 years until the complete decay.

About the Author

In 1985 Iraq's air force soon began strategic bombing against Iranian cities, chiefly Tehran. I was a little boy at that time, living with my family in the capital. After waiting for sometimes for bombing to stop, my parents decided to leave our house and go to another northern city which Saddam's air force couldn't bomb. One day we were in my grandparents' house and they bombed closed to their place, the amount of the wave and sound from the explosion impact me harshly and I couldn't talk for a while. They were a lot of children at that time which became mute. Not all saw the war in negative terms. The Islamic Revolution of Iran was strengthened and radicalized. The Iranian government-owned Etelaat newspaper wrote:

"There is not a single school or town that is excluded from the happiness of "Holy Defence" of the nation, from drinking the exquisite elixir of martyrdom, or from the sweet death of the martyr, who dies in order to live forever in paradise."

First when I went to college I was still in Iran and my field was Civil Engineering .pretty cool field still like it. Because I wanted to continue studying in Computer fields, That's why one of my best options became India which colleges are pretty eligible for Com Fields and Progressing in IT and computer field with the speed of light.

Love for the nature is with me from the childhood and when I came to India start to study photography and taking shots through years while my computer studying, mostly Macro Shots. How I got to Macro Photography field, not sure but probably because I used to get inspiring results, this is one of the main reasons. I always had to focus and zoom on one particular mostly small subject as Macro photographers do. The whole concept had an effect on my life after sometime and made me who I am now and change the way to concentrate on a subject.